THE BLUE IN ME

By

Rod Grimes

COPYRIGHTS

Printed in the United States of America

Published by Authorssolution.com

DISCLAIMER

The names and addresses in this book have been changed to protect the privacy of individuals. Any resemblance to real persons or locations is purely coincidental.

DEDICATION

My twenty-five-year career with the Detroit Police Department came to an end more than twenty years ago. I still reflect back with vivid memories of the good times as well as the heartbreaking times. My experiences and the people I met will forever be a part of my life.

Three years ago, I decided to write this book to provide others with an inside view of my professional life. More importantly I wanted to give my granddaughter some detailed information of what her grandpa did to make a difference.

This book, “The Blue In Me,” is the memoir of the first 25 years of my career; names and addresses have been changed to protect the privacy of those who crossed my path in various ways.

To Maia Grimes, my beautiful granddaughter, granddad loves you more than you can ever imagine. I dedicate this book to you as you were my inspiration for its creation.

To my mother, Emma Grimes, thank you for all the sacrifices you made throughout your life; I thank you for filling me with strong values and integrity to be successful and always encouraging me to be the best I can be at whatever I do.

To my father, Ive Grimes; you left this earthly life in 1996. However, you live daily in my heart, as well as so many of our treasured father-son talks.

For my readers, who breathe life into these pages. To all those who pick up this book, thank you for giving my words a chance. For every reader who finds a piece of themselves within these chapters. To the ones reading this book, may you find a new appreciation for the men and women working in law enforcement.

I thank God for this book-writing blessing.

ACKNOWLEDGMENTS

I extend my heartfelt gratitude to WriterClique for their unwavering support and guidance. Special thanks to Ted Baker and Adam Smith for their invaluable contributions to this book. Your impact is deeply appreciated.

Forward By
ROBERT DARNELL LEE

When I first met Rod Grimes, I wasn't sure how to take him. My first encounter with Rod was a car ride from Detroit, Michigan, to Dayton, Ohio; we were traveling there to compete in the law enforcement National Softball Championship Tournament.

I was a new guy on this up and coming national powerhouse team; Rod was the leader/captain, and the third guy in the car was Tony Mitchell and most responsible for me being added to the roster.

It is said first impressions are lasting, in this case, I am glad my first impression lasted the whole weekend. The three of us were roommates. I knew of several of the players but not personally, Rod included.

During that weekend, I got to know a lot about Rod, in addition to watching him perform at an extremely high level on the ball field. Rod's leadership skills were on full display; he led by example and I am not just talking about on the ball field. This man understood motivating people at their level then raising their bar.

Our time off the field was most gratifying; Tony was off doing what he enjoys, whereas Rod and I rather relaxed in the room. We talked about so much, the job, family relationships and so much more. The person I met was not the person I expected. This man is well grounded with strong family values and a caring heart.

Someone who believes in working hard to be successful, never looking for a handout or a shortcut. This man has a giving spirit and understands we are put on earth to utilize the talent God blessed us with to uplift others and have a positive impact on humanity.

To watch Rod on the ball field, his demeanor was so intense it could be mistaken for raw anger, but that was not the case at all; it was just his strong will to be successful. Once the game was over, won or lost, his sportsmanship always shone brightest.

Rod would be the first to congratulate the other team with a good game and a handshake. By the end of that weekend, I got to know a man of honor, integrity, and a giving heart.

That weekend was the beginning of a friendship stronger than most; over the years, I watched Roderick's career advance upward, from working with the Mayor to assisting the Deputy Chief before retiring as a sergeant.

Roderick accepted a police officer position with the Detroit Public School Police Department and quickly began to rise in the ranks, including making the rank of sergeant, then two years later being appointed to Chief of Police.

Leadership has been in Roderick's career path his whole life; as you read this book and future books detailing his interesting career, you will come to know the true leader he is, and more importantly, you will get to know an amazing man.

TABLE OF CONTENTS

Prologue

Growing up in the city of Detroit in the 60's and 70's was a fun and exciting time for this young black kid. The 60's provided me the opportunity to experience things that my older siblings couldn't experience. Being ten years old in the mid 60's was so different than for my sisters being ten years old in the 50's, only ten years apart but there were many things that were now accepted, like riding my bike in different neighborhoods, going in stores without a parent, and not be questioned by staff. Feeling accepted in our American culture in ways that were unthinkable for a black kid in the 50's.

During the 40's and 50's, Black Bottom was the community where more than a third of blacks were forced to live due to the huge economic divide between blacks and whites. My dad came to Detroit in the late 30's and spent his early years there. By the late 40's, he had been hired at Chrysler Corporation. His hard work and vision to have a better life for his family allowed him to move to an area nearby, which was known as Conant Gardens. A small neighborhood many blacks migrated to near the Chrysler plant.

In the early 50's my dad had fathered two children and was raising one, my oldest sister Ladeen. The mother of his first son had left Detroit with my brother Benjamin, moving to Mobile, Alabama. In 1951, my dad went to Memphis, Tennessee, where he found his high school sweetheart and moved her and her two children back to Detroit and married, creating a blended family.

Three years later, they birthed my brother Eugene, and in 1956, I was born into that marriage. Being the youngest of six kids had several perks, mainly I learned from their mistakes and was spared trips to the basement where dad flashed the leather to the butts of my siblings.

By the early 60's, divorce had found its way into my parent's marriage, which also included some prison time for my dad. Life was difficult for my mother, who was trying to raise five kids. Not long after my father's incarceration, my oldest sister became pregnant, delivered my niece shortly after graduating high school, left our home, and moved to California to be with her birth mother.

My mother was forced to go on government assistance (welfare and ADC) Aid to Dependent Children. Her struggles were many. She had foregone completing her college education while in Memphis and started a family with my older sibling's dad, which failed. She then survived a controlling husband in my dad's life. Mom was forced to take on part-time service jobs, like counter person at diners during the day and janitorial jobs at night.

By now, you may be asking yourself what was so great about growing up in those conditions. Although socially, we were considered poor, for the most part, I didn't relate to that status. Although we may have moved several times between ages 6 and 16, we always live in the northeast section of the city, usually mixed neighborhoods.

Having the opportunity to play sports was a huge distraction from the lack of financial means. At ages eight and six, Eugene and I went to work with my mother at her janitorial job and earned a few dollars each week by dumping the trash cans.

By age 16, and once I earned my driver's license, I was hired on by the company and began earning my own check. These valuable lessons learned early in life began to mold me while building a sound work ethic.

Life was good and continued to be, as you will read about my journey in my chosen profession, Law Enforcement.

Chapter 1
Follow Your Dreams

My parents always taught me to follow my dreams wherever they took me to be the best I could be in what I did. It is summertime 1962; I am a 6-year-old, swinging on the monkey bars at the corner playground, when I noticed some of the older boys from the neighborhood playing a game. One boy stood with a stick and attempted to hit a ball thrown by another boy. In an instant, I was totally captivated by the skills they were displaying. This game had my full attention. I climbed down off the monkey bars and sat quietly against the fence, close enough to the action but far enough away not to be in the field of play or, for that matter, even be noticed. Within minutes, I began to understand the concept of the game. One team would hit the ball while the other team, wearing very large gloves on one hand, would attempt to catch the ball, and then they would switch sides. I sat there all afternoon watching this now very exciting game, which I later learned was called baseball.

When I returned home that day, I asked my dad to tell me what he knew about the game called baseball. My dad sat down in his favorite chair; I sat on the floor at his feet. He began to explain this game as I sat there wide-eyed and excited. After what seemed like hours, he said, "It's time for dinner." I replied, "No, please tell me more," but dinner won over.

For the next few years, my life centered on learning everything I could about my future career as a professional baseball player.

At age 10, I had a neighbor (Ronnie) who was 5 years older than me. Because of my love for the game of baseball, he would take me to all of his practices, and I got to learn from kids 5, 7, and even 8 years older than me because he was playing on a team where most players were a couple of years older than him. The team adopted me as their junior teammate and bat boy.

Ronnie was the team's shortstop. He was like a magician on the field, and he was the Wizard of Oz before that guy from the St. Louis Cardinals ever came on the scene. Ronnie was my childhood baseball hero and I wanted to be just like him.

Shortly before my 12th birthday, Ronnie was tragically killed. Like me, all Ronnie ever wanted to do was play baseball and, hopefully, one day play professionally. Ronnie had an older brother, James, and his life was going in a very different direction. James began using and then pushing drugs. One night, after James had stiffed some guys in a drug deal, the guys showed up at their house looking for him and when they couldn't locate James, they took Ronnie instead. Two days later, James was contacted and told where he could find Ronnie's body. Ronnie had been abducted and executed, two rounds to the head and left in an abandoned warehouse near the Detroit River. I was devastated; my closest friend and baseball mentor had been taken away from me for no reason. I share that story for two reasons. First, my parents always told me when I found something I loved doing, I committed to it, and that's what I did with Ronnie's help. Secondly, the murder of Ronnie made me want to someday become a police officer and find the people responsible for killing Ronnie. Within a few months after Ronnie's death, the two men responsible for killing him were arrested.

The next eight years passed and I had been a baseball standout in high school and on the sandlots. I had a few looks from professional teams, but that dream ended with a knee injury at the age of 20. With a baseball career clearly in my rear-view mirror, I focused on my education as I had enrolled in college following graduating high school.

One day, while sitting in my accounting class, the thought of working behind a desk, crunching numbers as an accountant, I knew that could no longer be my career path. After school that day, I went to the Detroit Police Department's Recruiting Office and applied for the position of police officer.

I called it a position and not a job because the title of police officer in my book means service to the community; it is so much more than just a job. It's a profession and a profession that requires dedication and total commitment. With a passion for serving in my community and a dedication to performing at a high level, this was my true calling.

Chapter 2
Training Day

February 20, 1978, the first day in the academy, I am 21 years old and ready to save the world. It wasn't long before my leadership characteristics began to show. I was the one always encouraging others to push a little harder during physical training, building team unity, or working thru problem-solving drills. I was selected by the Training Command Staff to lead my class into the auditorium carrying the American flag during graduation ceremonies, which is the highest honor bestowed on an officer in training.

A police department is a para-military operation, and because of the tremendous responsibility placed on those who choose this profession, the training is long, hard and detailed. The power and authority of a police officer in the state of Michigan is greater than the state itself, whereas, under certain circumstances, an officer can take the life of a citizen.

Twelve weeks have passed, and it's graduation day; 63 cadets have started, but only 43 have survived the intense training. The last words from our training sergeant were, "Keep your head down and ears open. There is so much more for you to learn and the streets will teach you."

Then came the time to hear our assignments. Let me just say that all we heard about during the 12 weeks of training were horror stories about the department's 5th Precinct - Precinct 5, the highest crime district in the city, Precinct 5, the most racist district in the city among its officers. Remember, this is just a little more than 10 years after the deadliest race riots in America. Clearly, no one wanted to be assigned to Precinct 5. The sergeant began reading off the assignments. Fourteen names are called before he gets to my name and no one has been assigned to Precinct 5. "Grimes," the sergeant barks out, "Precinct Five." All eyes are now looking at me, waiting for some kind of reaction. Without thought or hesitation, I snapped a stern salute in acknowledgment. "Sir, I won't disappoint you." By the time all the assignments were given out, four officers were assigned to Precinct 5, including Officer White, who had become a close friend during our training.

"Officer White," I said, "now that we are both assigned to the same Precinct, wouldn't it be great if we were assigned to the same shift." He replied, "What would be even crazier, if we could eventually become partners."

Chapter 3
Reporting For Duty

It's Monday morning and the first day to report to our new assignment. I walk down the hallway towards the roll call room; my stomach knotted from the feeling of not knowing what to expect from my new colleagues. As I approached the door, I saw there were about 30 officers staring at me. To my pleasant surprise, there are eight faces I know from high school or from playing baseball over the years. Oh wow, it's homecoming!

The excitement was racing at an all-time high, and then the shift lieutenant and three sergeants entered the roll call room. One sergeant gave the order to fall in for roll call. "Two ranks," he barked. I am thinking to myself, "Boy, its official. I am a police officer. Let's get going, time to serve and protect." After the roll call, the other newbies and I were sent to see the Patrol Inspector for orientation. As we filed into the Inspector's office, to my surprise, he was a black man. I was thinking how bad could it be around here. My shift Lieutenant and his boss, the Patrol Inspector, are both black.

The Inspector greeted us with a welcome and what came with that was a strong smell of mouthwash working overtime trying to cover the odor of alcohol. Clearly, this man has a drinking problem, I concluded. For the next two hours, we had to endure war stories about his career. The stories weren't bad, but the smell was hard to take. My first opinion of my second highest-ranking executive in the Precinct was not a favorable one. Could this be the reason for some of the issues going on at this precinct?

Now it's time to hit the streets; a scout car arrived at the station to transport us out to our beat. We all pile into the back seat of the patrol car that was parked in front of the building, and the next thing I know, the officer driving activates the emergency lights and siren and away we go. "Wow!" I am thinking, "All of this just to take us out to walk a beat." He makes a right turn, drives the wrong way down a one-way street and whips the car partially to the curb. He jumps out of the car and says, "Come on. This is a 'cut in.'" Now, I am sure I was paying attention during my academy training, and although I never heard the term "cut in" as a radio code, I am following along as if I knew what the heck was going on.

We all entered into a house and in the front room, lying on a couch, was a gentleman bleeding from the chest area. I now realized the officer was saying that the nature of the call was a "cutting." The lead officer asked what happened, and the man stated, "My neighbor next door and close friend for over thirty years did this to me." When asked why, the gentleman replied, "We were arguing over who the rightful owner was of a bamboo fishing pole." I knew from this moment going forward, I would not let anything I saw or heard shock or amaze me. A few minutes later, another scout car crew arrived and took over the investigation.

The officer driving took us to a busy intersection and told us to get out of his car while muttering, "For the rest of the shift just walk around in this area and when it's time, I will come back and pick you up."

Each day was another adventure. For the next few weeks, I walked a beat and was partnered with one of my classmates. As a 22-year-old, I was six foot, three inches tall, weighing 215 pounds, and in great shape. My partner, Officer Williams, was a 5'3" white female who may have weighed 125 pounds with all of her gear on. I often wondered how she would handle herself in a real fight. Don't get me wrong, she had done okay in the academy, but let's be real, that is a controlled environment. As I stated earlier, we were in the highest crime area in the city and many of the citizens didn't care for the police, especially white officers.

We got to know several of the business owners as they were very happy to see officers walking the beat in the area. Restaurant, party store and gas station owners were always encouraging us to stop in their establishments to get out of the rain or giving us something to eat or munch on, but we knew they just really wanted the police on location for security reasons.

Somehow, I knew it wouldn't be long before we were challenged by some of the local knuckleheads, and sure enough, it happened. The second week on the beat patrol, three young guys were walking on the opposite side of the street and when they noticed us, they crossed over to our side. I immediately started sizing them up. I knew this was trouble walking at us. As they passed by, one of the guys bumped my partner with an aggressive shoulder bump and stated, "Bitch this is my sidewalk and when you see me coming, get the hell out of my way." Before I could respond, my partner grabbed the youngster, gave him an open-hand heel strike to the nose, and slammed him to the ground shouting, "Listen you little shit. Today is your lucky day, because I am not going to kick your ass and take you to jail, but understand this. This is my sidewalk and you are laying on it bleeding and I want you off it." I looked at the other two guys and said, "If you don't want some of that, I suggest you get to stepping." The one bleeding guy pulled himself up off the ground, and they all jogged away.

A crowd of about 20 people had gathered to watch, and after the young men had run away, the crowd started clapping and cheering. I heard one person say, "Thank you officers. That's just the kind of action we need around here. These youngsters think they are in charge." It was at that moment I knew I was in the right profession; the citizens really appreciated the police and were willing to support us if needed.

Chapter 4
Best Partner Ever

The calendar has changed and I am now working the 4:00 pm to midnight shift. I spent the last four days on leave and finally, I am back at work and very excited. Today is even more special because I am partnered with my good friend from the academy, Officer Dion White. Dion I and I were probably the two toughest guys in our class. We were ready to go out and clean up the city; well, at least the problems on the beat that we were patrolling. A couple of hours into the shift, we stopped a guy for jaywalking, yes, jaywalking. We had to start somewhere. Officer White yelled at the guy crossing mid-block, interfering with vehicular traffic. "Stop right there!" We walked over to him and White asked him for identification. The 20-something-year-old looked in disbelief that he was being stopped by the police for jaywalking. The guy had no identification on him. Officer White told him to put his hands on the wall of the building and began to pat him down. "What's this?" my partner asked as he felt a large bulge in his front right pocket. The guy pulled out a wad of money, which had to be at least seven or eight hundred dollars. "What's this in your other pocket?" and out came a plastic baggie filled with crack rocks, about 50 to 60. "Hands behind your back," and just like that, we had made our first drug arrest.

The next day, Dion and I are partners again. We made our way out to our beat via the city bus. Most of the officers that were assigned to walking a beat would wait around the station for a patrol unit to give them a ride, but we wanted to get out there as soon as possible. Lucky for us, the beat we were assigned to was only three miles away from the station, straight down Jefferson Ave.

There was a mini-station located on every beat, so the officers had somewhere to go during the shift to take a break and get off their feet.

Our day has been uneventful, other than writing a few parking tickets. The sun has set, and more people are out along the strip.

Dion and I decided to take another walk just to make our presence known. It usually took about an hour to make a full trip around, and we were only a block away from the mini-station when a city bus pulled up and the front doors opened. The bus driver yells, "Hey guys, how's it going? Do you want a ride?" I responded, "No, we are good. We just made a round and we are only a block away from our mini-station." The driver asks again. "Come on, take a ride with me." Again, I told him no, that we were good, but maybe next time. The driver says, "Well, I need you guys to come on the bus for a minute. I am having a little problem with one of the riders." All damn! I missed the hint he was trying to give us.

I stepped on the bus first, with Officer White following me. The driver said the guy in the black jacket had been cursing and threatening other passengers. I walked towards the back of the bus, stopped at the passenger in the black jacket and told him, "Sir, I need you to step off the bus." He responded by sticking his hand inside his jacket as if he was reaching for something. I quickly drew my gun from my holster and placed the barrel against his forehead and said, "Pull your hand out of your jacket and if anything comes out other than your hand, I will blow your fucking head off."

He complied and his hand came out empty. I told him to get up as the bus driver opened the rear door. The guy stood up, and he had to be over 7 feet tall. I thought, "Oh shit," but I just grabbed him and threw him down the steps of the rear door. He grabbed my arm as he went flying out the door and onto the ground with me in tow. Officer White came out behind us, along with an unknown female following White. I am on top; both of us are throwing punches. My punches are much more effective because I have the leverage. White is now in the mix as we attempt to handcuff this guy. The female tries to assist him by attempting to stab me with a pointed umbrella, but Dion, from his knees, pulls his nightstick and whacks her across the chest. She takes off running through the crowd that had gathered.

Dion, not knowing how the crowd was going to react to this situation, got his radio out and called for assistance. In a matter of what seemed like only a few seconds, Jefferson Ave was filled with police cars. My combatant was cuffed, placed into a patrol car, and transported to the station. Dion and I were given a ride by another crew, and while on the way to the station, I was thinking, "WOW! How fast things can go from sugar to shit, and boy, the backup got there so fast, almost as if they were falling out of the sky."

Chapter 5
Foolish Chase

The summertime festivals were in full swing, and each district had to send a number of officers downtown to work the details. It was a no-brainier that the rookie officers would be sent because the older veteran officers wanted no part of chasing the purse snatchers and the gang banger who often show up at these events. It's Sunday afternoon. I had just completed my 7:00 am to 3:00 pm shift and was ready to head home to relax. I pulled out of the parking lot in my personal vehicle and stopped at the traffic light. As I sat there watching a large crowd cross the street, I thought, "Boy, there's going to be thousands of people here this evening." The traffic light turned green and just as I began to move, I heard a car accelerating, trying to make it through the light. I stopped, but the motorcycle rider next to me kept going, and BAM, the speeding car, t-boned the motorcycle.

"Damn!" that biker is going to be hurt pretty bad, the driver of the car kept going. "What the hell!" I know the driver had to have known he hit that guy. I began following the vehicle, attempting to wave him down and get him to stop. The driver was completely ignoring me as he entered the freeway. I continued to follow him for several miles until he exited the freeway and turned onto a residential street, pulling to the curb. I pulled next to him and jumped out of my vehicle, gun drawn, ordering him to turn off the vehicle and toss the keys into the street.

Several people were outside enjoying the warm summer day. I yelled for someone to dial 911 and advise the operator that an off-duty uniform officer was holding a subject at gunpoint for Hit and Run and was requesting assistance.

Three minutes later, the street was filled with police cars and the driver was taken into custody. I followed the scout car to the station and advised the desk sergeant of what I had witnessed and my actions that followed. The Sergeant took me back to his room and began giving me an earful. "Why the hell are you chasing vehicles while off duty and driving your personal car? You know I should write you up for that shit, don't you?" The Sergeant then directed me to begin my follow-up investigation. "You brought this shit into my district; you are going to handle all of the paperwork that goes with it, rookie or not." Just as I thought it couldn't get any worse, it did! After calling downtown to the communication section to find out what hospital the victim was conveyed to, I was told no EMS unit had been dispatched to that location for an injury accident. WHAT!!! How could that be? I had watched the biker go flying through the air and land in the middle of the street. Furthermore, no other officer had reported any type of accident from that location. I called all of the hospitals in the area. Nope, no biker is being treated here from an accident, was the answer I received over and over.

This is a problem; I have arrested someone but don't have a complainant. My saving grace was after running the driver in the system, I found he not only was driving on a suspended license, but he also had a few arrest warrants for assault, so much for a relaxing evening. By the time I finished all the paperwork, it was 11:45 pm.

Chapter 6
No Backup

Fall has arrived and I had gotten my feet wet, even if it was walking the beat most days. I had only seen the inside of a patrol car about eight or ten times. One day, my shift Lieutenant called me to the side after roll call and asked if I was any good at playing basketball. I replied that I was not a big scorer, but I was a very good defender and had strong rebounding skills. "Great," he replied. "We have practice tomorrow for the precinct basketball team. You will be working with Officer White and I will see that you guys are freed up to be there. "We are working a scout car together?" I asked with a loud, excited voice. "Yes, I will put you two rookies together and you had better not screw up." Then, he slightly smiles and says, "You guys will be fine."

Tuesdays and Thursdays were practice days for the team, and the Lieutenant made sure I was partnered with Officer White. Our dream had come true. We were not only assigned to the same precinct and on the same shift, but we were also partners two days out of the week. We had died and gone to heaven.

Then it happened: racism began to rear its ugly head. Whenever Officer White and I worked together, it required the Lieutenant to move some of the veteran officers to other assignments, and they were having no part of it. The veteran officers filed a union grievance against the Lieutenant, and I was sure my days working with Officer White would end. The Precinct Commander heard the complaint and supported the Lieutenant's decision, questioning why we weren't together every day. You see, whenever White and I worked together, we produced the highest stats on the shift, even though we were only in service for five and a half hours of the eight-hour shift. The Commander even made a point of coming to one of our shift's roll calls, something that rarely happens at our precinct. The Commander was a man of few words, but the troops knew when he spoke, all ears had better be open. He talked about productivity and how many of the veteran officers should be ashamed of letting a couple of young rookies outperform them. "As a matter of fact," he shouted, "you should be downright EMBARRASSED!" It was clear to me the point he was trying to drive home to the more seasoned officers, but it had an adverse effect on Officer White and myself.

Once roll call was over and we were getting our gear to hit the streets, more than a few of the vets let us know that they were not happy with us. We heard comments like, "So you guys think you are real police. Rookies don't last very long around here when they don't stay in their place," to name a few.

It didn't take long to clearly understand what they meant. Many of the old-timers had friends working down at dispatch, and it is amazing how far a six-pack of beer would go when asking for a favor from them. Instantly, White and I began receiving all of the slop calls. It was stuff that would keep us tied up for hours but had no real action, just a lot of paperwork, which meant we would not be available to generate high-volume arrests and ticket stats.

Officer White and I refused to let them win. We both were of the mindset that when you have lemons, make lemonade.

Over the radio, our first call of the day, "scout 5-8. Make 2275 Garland. Meet the woman on a report of a missing dog."

Within minutes, we were on location, getting the information on the missing dog. As we began our patrol around the area, looking for the missing German Shepherd mixed with an unknown breed, over the air comes a high priority call. "Scout 5-3. Attention cars in #5. 13415 Kercheval reports of shots fired. Someone may be shot inside that location." I tell my partner, "Let's go. That address is only a few blocks away." We were the first unit to arrive on the scene and people were running everywhere; clearly, something had just happened here.

As I am exiting the patrol car and notifying the dispatcher scout. 5-8 is on location at 13415 Kercheval; I see a young black male on the ground near the side of the house. He is holding his stomach with both hands while trying to get back on his feet. Blood was covering his hands and shirt. I draw my weapon and move in his direction. My partner heads towards the front door.

"Radio scout 5-8," I yell into the mic on my hand-held radio. "We have one person shot at this location, and we need EMS, ASAP." The next thing I knew, my partner was on the porch fighting with a guy, attempting to run from the house. A quick right hand from my partner and the guy was down on his back. "Roll over and put your hands behind your back motherfucker," White screams at the man. The scene is chaotic. A lady appears from I don't know where, shouting, "My brother is in the house and he has been shot." "Holy shit," I am thinking. "What have we gotten ourselves into?" "Radio scout 5-8," I yell into the mic again. "We have another person shot at this location. We will need a second EMS unit, and where are the other units? We need some help over here!" The Dispatcher replied, "Calm down officer. More units are en route, and I will order a second medical unit for you."

Suddenly, I could hear what sounded like half the police department's sirens, and they were getting louder. Seconds later, one car pulls up, then another, and another. Within a couple of minutes, the block was filled with police cars, no less than a dozen. It took only minutes for us to gain control of the scene. Three people had been shot, but the shooter had already run from the house before our arrival. The guy on the porch White had detained was a cousin of one of the shooting victims. He was attempting to chase after the shooter but didn't want to explain that to my partner and landed himself in handcuffs.

When the Sergeant arrived on location, things had calmed down considerably. "Grimes/White, get over here!" he barked, calling us to his patrol car. "So, you think you know how to get shit done do you? Well, this is your scene. Now handle it, rookies!" Then he turned away, got into his car, and drove off. Slowly, one by one, the police cars began to leave the scene. Within five minutes after the Sergeant had pulled away, there was only one other car there with us. The officers who stayed behind with us also played on the basketball team. Both officers are white; one stated, "We got your back BROTHER."

Needless to say, it took us the rest of the shift and a couple of hours in overtime to make all the notifications, wait for the homicide unit and evidence team to arrive, then go to the hospital and get statements from the victims. Unfortunately, one didn't make it.

We went back to the station and completed all of the paperwork.

The next day, roll call was being conducted by Sergeant Kowcowski, the same Sergeant who had made our scene the day before. After the assignments were given out, he barked out, "Grimes/White!" "Oh shit!" I'm thinking. "He is about to reem our asses for yesterday." "Good job officers," he stated. "Other than you screaming on the radio like a girl, Grimes, you rookies did a good job out there." That brought a laugh from most of the officers. Noticeably, the female officers didn't find any humor in his statement. "Give these rookies a hand," the Sergeant directed the troops. The applause was lackluster, at best.

Several months went by without Officer White and me getting very much backup on high-priority calls, but we took it in stride. No way were we going to let them feel like they broke us and think we couldn't handle ourselves out there on the street.

That didn't stop us from showing up on their calls and backing them up. Finally, one day after our shift was over, a group of veteran officers walked up to us in the parking lot. I was thinking, "WOW! Really, are we now going to have to fight with them?" Thank goodness that was not the case. One of the officers said, "You two guys are alright. You know how to handle your shit out there on the streets." Don't get me wrong, they weren't about to teach us the secret handshake, but at least now they were willing to back us up on calls.

Chapter 7
Officer Down

Two years have passed. White and I have really settled into our careers and life is good. It's a sunny fall Thursday afternoon around 4:45 pm. We had just hit the streets and, as always, began making our cruise through our patrol area, checking on the hot spots when dispatch came on the air. "All UNITS, All UNITS! Mack Ave. and Conner Ave. We are receiving information of an off-duty officer down in the Burger King parking lot." "Damn, damn, damn!" my partner yells as he accelerates to a high speed. I flick on the emergency lights and hit the siren; we are about three miles away. Traffic is heavy because of rush hour and it seems like it is taking us forever to get there, but in reality, Officer White got us there in about two and a half minutes. The intersection and Burger King parking lot were already filled with police vehicles. EMS is also pulling up behind us. I told White to leave our scout car in the left turn lane. I jumped out to let the EMS driver know to position his rig behind us, and we would be the lead car going to the hospital.

We ran over to the crowd of officers, and sure enough, the off-duty officer had been shot in the lower back and leg. The EMS crew began giving him the medical attention needed as one of the first officers on the scene was trying to ascertain what had happened. No supervisor had arrived on site yet, and everyone was just standing around. I yell out, "Second, third and fourth units on scene, start canvasing the customers inside the restaurant and people at the bus stop to see if anyone saw what happened. Fifth unit on scene, start putting up crime scene tape to secure the area, then start making the proper notifications within the department. Everyone else, get in your patrol cars and start blocking off the main intersections all the way to St. John's Hospital, which is about five miles away."

The EMS crew got the officer loaded into the wagon; I notified the dispatcher we were rolling and to contact the hospital and let them know we were coming in HOT, eta four minutes. Traffic was held by all the units as requested and we zipped down the center lane all the way to the hospital.

Our part was done, and we headed back to our patrol area. The rest of our shift was uneventful and that was a good thing. As it turns out, the off-duty officer had been shot by some guy trying to rob him.

As police officers, we respond to all types of calls. The worst are those involving kids and injured officers.

Our shift was over and I was headed to the door towards my car. My Lieutenant stops me and says, "I need a minute with you Grimes."

We walked back to his office, and he told me to take a seat. "Um." I am thinking. "What's going on here?" The Lieutenant asks me why I thought I had the right to give officers instructions. "You are not a supervisor, especially at a shooting scene involving a police officer." He continues, saying those types of events should be handled by seasoned supervisors. "Yes sir, I understand, but there were no supervisors on scene and everyone was just standing around doing nothing. I knew something had to be done and someone had to take the lead so I stepped up and did what I knew needed to be done. I may not have gotten everything right sir, but I couldn't just stand around with my head up my butt. If I messed up, I am ready to accept my discipline." "On the contrary,

Grimes." the Lieutenant said with a wry smile. "You did an outstanding job out there today. When the first Sergeant arrived on scene, he advised me that he thought another supervisor was there." "One last thing," the Lieutenant said. "I want you to start studying for the Sergeant's promotional exam. I think you have a future as a leader in this department."

For the next hour, we sat there and talked shop. The Lieutenant was schooling me on the ins and outs of becoming a supervisor. He was sitting in his chair in a very relaxed manner and just giving me all kinds of police situation scenarios, and I was soaking up every word. Week after week the Lieutenant would pull me into his office, and we would have informal supervisor training sessions. One day, as I was leaving the station, a couple of the older white officers stopped me in the parking lot. "So, I hear you are the Lieutenant's 'little bitch', and he is trying to help get you promoted," one of the officers said. I was in the mood for a confrontation, so I replied, "Somebody has to want to take the lead. Everybody can't just walk around here with their thumb up their ass, waiting to be told what to do every step of the way. So yes, I am learning what it takes to become a supervisor. I came on this job to make it a career and to make a difference in this city. The way I see it, part of making a difference will be changing the mindset of officers like the two of you or doing what it takes to get your asses shipped out of here." I pushed my way past them and walked over to my car.

Things have settled down around the station. All the bullshit and bickering has found its way to the back burner. Most of the officers are here just trying to get the job done and go home safe to their families. Officer White and I are both putting in the hours studying for the promotional exam. We're constantly quizzing one another while out on patrol.

Chapter 8
Stolen Thunderbird

Over the radio came the sound of the dispatcher, "Radio calling scout 5-8." Officer White grabbed the mic and responded, "5-8 radio go ahead." We received a call to a home in a very affluent neighborhood in our precinct. We arrived on the scene and spoke with a middle-aged woman who was very upset that her car had been stolen. She kept saying the car was the only thing she had ever bought with her own money, further stating that her husband was the breadwinner in their home and she was a housewife in the true sense of the title. Officer White took all the information about the 1973 white Ford Thunderbird; it took a minute to pull the info out of her as she was so distraught she could barely speak. I asked her several times if there was anything about her vehicle that would make it stand out from any other white Thunderbird's; as we were leaving, she mentioned that the headlights had half-moon silver covers over them. We advised her that a stolen car report would be filed and patrol units would be looking out for it. She replied, "Yeah right, I'm sure you officers have much more important things to do than look for my stolen vehicle," and the tears began to rain down like a waterfall. Officer White and I headed back to the station, knocked out the stolen car report, and finished the remainder of our shift without anything exciting happening.

As we were driving home, just a couple of blocks away from White's house, I noticed a white Thunderbird pass me going in the opposite direction. I stopped speaking in mid-sentence as I was quizzing White on a possible exam question and asked him if he saw the Thunderbird that had just passed us. "It was white and it had half-moon silver headlight covers over the lights." I whipped a U-turn as Officer White dug for the pocket notepad where he had taken the information about the stolen car down.

I have now caught up with the white Thunderbird but keep a little distance between us, not wanting to spook the driver. White is frantically rifling through the pages, looking for his notes. The vehicle is occupied by two males, and the driver is driving normally. The fact that we were in my personal car didn't bring about any suspicion. "Here it is," White says finally, and sure as shit, this is the stolen white Ford Thunderbird we had taken the report on just a few hours earlier from the other side of town. WOW!!! "What are we going to do?" White asked me. "There is not much we can do other than follow them and hope we will see a police car driving by that we can flag down to assist."

The driver makes a right turn, and then a few blocks later, he makes a left turn. "Damn," I think. "He may know someone is following him, but he continues to drive at a normal speed." "Where are the police when you need them?" is the thought that crossed my mind. We have been following them for what seems to have been 10 minutes, and still no police car in sight. Finally, the driver turns down a residential street; the street lights are not working. The driver pulls slowly to the curb near a playground. I tell White to get ready because I think they are about to bail and run. I whipped in behind them, and we both jumped out with guns drawn. I yelled for the driver to turn the vehicle off and for the passenger to slowly open his door and come out and lay face down on the ground. Both complied with those instructions. Next, I ordered the driver to slide across the seat, come out the passenger door and lay face down. Thank God we got both of them out of the car without incident, got them cuffed, and seated on the curb.

I heard a male voice coming from one of the homes across the street, "Hey, what the hell is going on out here?" I responded, "Sir, there are two off-duty police officers over here. We just stopped two guys in a stolen vehicle. Please go back inside and dial 911 and advise the operator that there are off-duty officers holding two suspects at gunpoint in front of your house." The male voice replied, "Right away." Moments later I heard the voice say, "I called, and the operator said someone will be here shortly."

Five minutes and no police cars. "What the hell is going on?" I am thinking. "That type of call going into police communications should have had the cavalry here in no time," I asked the gentleman to call back and repeat what he had told the operator before. Moments later, I heard the male say, "I called back, and they told me that officers should be here any minute." I thanked him again. Now, more than ten minutes have passed since we got these guys out of the vehicle, and I can tell that although they were handcuffed, they were getting antsy. I asked the male voice to call back one more time and, this time, tell the operator that the officers were now in trouble. About a minute later, I could hear the sirens in the distance getting closer. Two police cars came squealing around the corner and the officers jumped out, guns drawn. One officer yelled, "Sorry guys we took so long, but we are the only two units working in our precinct tonight and we were at a large fight at a bar when your call for help came out." "I am glad you guys made it." Off to jail for the two car thieves.

Later that night I called the owner and shared with her the good news about finding her vehicle. Now, the tears of sadness turned to tears of joy.

Chapter 9
Everybody Is Going To Jail Today

Today is shift change and we are rotating to the afternoon shift. Bummer! It usually takes two weeks to get adjusted to a new sleeping pattern. Oh well, that's part of the job. My regular partner, Officer White, is taking vacation for the first 10 days, so I will be working with different partners almost every day until he returns.

Summertime in the Motor City can be hot in more ways than one. The temperature is 92 degrees with about 70% humidity. Yes, it's a HOT one today and we still don't have air conditioning in the patrol cars. I arrived at the station in a very foul mood because my girlfriend and I had a silly argument about me not being interested in attending her cousin's birthday party tonight. I don't get off work until midnight and that's if I don't have to stay for overtime. I just want to go home and unwind. I insisted that she would be going without me. Nevertheless, I was still pretty pissed off as I sat in the roll call room awaiting roll call.

As the room began to fill with other officers and the Sergeant walked to the front, I announced in a very authoritative voice, "I am pissed off and it is hot as hell out there. I'm not taking no shit today. Everybody is going to jail." The room got quiet and the Sgt. just looked at me and shook his head. By the time roll call was over and we got our gear and made it to our patrol car, I was feeling much better. I was joking with one of the older officers about how his duty belt was beginning to sag under his belly and the fitness room was screaming his name every day.

Today, my partner is Officer Rice. He is a mountain of a man, six feet, eight inches tall and over 300 pounds with very little fat. He threw me the keys and said, "How about you drive?" "Okay, cool," I replied and jumped behind the wheel. The inside of our car is smothering hot and Officer Rice asked, "How about a slush from the Dairy Queen?" "Great idea," I responded. "Let's roll." We only made it three blocks from the station, and over the radio came, "scout 5-8, I need to show you en route to 5781 Lemay. Auto accident, no injuries." Damn! That cold slush will have to wait. Rice grabbed the mic and responded, "On the way 5-8." As we arrived on location, we noticed a large crowd; my partner said, "Let's watch our backs. These are the projects and we are not the most welcomed people here."

We began our investigation and quickly realized there would be an arrest. The driver of this one car accident was clearly drunk. On went the cuffs and into the back seat he went, and not a moment too soon. The crowd was quite upset with the driver as he had run up on the sidewalk and almost hit several young kids playing. The damage was significant as he had hit two parked cars before his vehicle came to rest against the stop sign.

I spoke with a woman who witnessed the whole thing. She began to describe what happened; the driver was originally a passenger in the car when it pulled up to the address down the street. The driver got out of the car and went into the house. A few minutes later, the passenger slid across the seat, got behind the wheel, started the car, and took off. She continued saying he was swerving, then hit two cars before running up on the sidewalk and almost striking the kids that were playing. "The only thing that stopped the vehicle was him hitting the stop sign," she said. "It's a good thing you officers got here as quick as you did because that crowd was about to do some physical harm to that guy for almost hitting those kids." I thanked the woman for giving me a statement and returned to the patrol car.

My partner had already started the report and called for the tow truck. I turned and asked Mr. Brooks, the person we had arrested in the back seat, why he had gotten behind the wheel of the car and started driving. He yelled several curse words at me and ended his statement by saying, "Because I was tired of waiting for that motherfucker who went inside to buy the dope." I replied, "Well you just got a free ride to jail." I was not ready for what happened next. Mr. Brooks and I use the term Mister loosely, hacked up a mouth full of spit and let me have it right on the back of my neck, and began to call me every name in the book. That was a bad move on his part. I calmly got out of the car, walked around to the rear door, opened it, and punched him in the face.

"Dammit!" I yelled because the punch opened his face, and blood squirted all over my shirt. Mr. Brooks was in la-la land, out like a light. I slammed the door shut and started to get back in the driver's seat as I heard a guy yelling down the street to most of the crowd that had moved away, "Damn, come look at what he just did to this guy's face!" The crowd reformed and I am thinking we need to get this wrapped up and get out of here before someone else does something stupid. There are about 25 people around our car and I hear someone ask, "Who did that? The big officer?" "No," replied the guy who saw what happened. "It was the little officer." "WOW! He is knocked the fuck out," I hear a voice from the crowd say. Then I hear someone else say, "The son of a bitch is lucky the cops came, otherwise he would have gotten much more than that. He needed his ass fucked up for what he did."

Finally, the tow truck pulled up and hooked the vehicle. Off to the station, we go. My partner opened the rear car door and shook

Mr. Brooks a few times, and he began to stir a bit. "Come on, get out Mr. Brooks," Officer Rice orders, and he complies. We walked into the lockup area and were greeted by the Sergeant. He takes one look at our prisoner and yells, "God dammit Grimes what happened?" I explained the circumstances of the accident and what happened once Mr. Brooks was placed in the back seat of our patrol car. The Sergeant stood quietly for a moment, then said, "Yes, I get it. This asshole," referring to Mr. Brooks, "got behind the wheel of the vehicle, started driving, hit two parked cars and a stop sign, hit his head on the windshield and suffered these injuries to his face, right?" I replied, "No Sir," and repeated that Mr. Brooks was in the back seat of our patrol car and decided to spit on me, and I punched him one time with a closed fist, causing his injuries. The Sergeant says, "Yes, that's what I said. This asshole got behind the wheel of the car, had an accident and hit his face on the windshield and sustained his injuries." "No Sgt. I get what you are trying to do; cover for me, but this asshole spit on me so I tried to knock his fucking head off. I realize I was wrong for hitting him while he was in handcuffs and unable to defend himself, but he got what I felt he needed at that moment." "Okay Grimes, if you want the official report to read that way, I will have to open an investigation on an injured prisoner." "Yes Sir. I am ready to accept any discipline that comes my way. I am owning all of that."

The Sergeant on patrol was directed to go over to the accident location and see if anyone would give a witness statement related to how Mr. Brooks' eye got split open. After booking Mr. Brooks into the system, my partner and I took Mr. Brooks to the hospital to have his cuts stitched up. The investigating sergeant (Sgt. Tyler) was back at the station when we arrived from the hospital. He shared with the Lieutenant that several people were willing to talk and tell what happened. All the witnesses agreed that the two cops were very professional and, as far as they were concerned, too nice to that guy. It was only when the guy spit on the officer that he got a little of what he needed because they wanted to do much more than just one punch. Mr. Brooks was interviewed by Sgt. Tyler also stated he was wrong for spitting on the officer; he got what he deserved and didn't want to make an issue out of it.

Chapter 10
Key To The City

Back on midnight's again, 12:00 am to 8:00 am. Oh well, this is part of what I signed up for. As we hit the streets, calls for service in our precinct are backed up with 42 calls waiting. "Well partner, it's going to be a busy night." Officer White replies, "Let's go make a difference." By two-thirty am, all the calls for service had been answered, and the police radio was quiet. White says, "Let's grab a bite to eat," and we head towards one of only three restaurants open in the area. Over the radio comes a call for scout 5-9, "2639 St. Jean, possible abduction in progress." "What do you think? Should we go back up that unit?" my partner asks. "Sure, why not?" We arrived on the scene; the crew was there, as well as one of our Sergeants.

It appeared that the grandmother had been babysitting. The mother was there to pick up the child, but the grandmother felt that the mother had been drinking and should not be driving, especially with the child in the car. Sergeant Jorgensen was talking to the grandmother through the door, explaining that he had interviewed the mother, found her fit to operate a vehicle and that she needed to turn the child over to the mother. The grandmother was having no part of that and refused to open the door and allow the mother to take the child. The Sergeant, all but begging grandma to release the child to the mother's care, finally got fed up and pissed off. "Look lady, if you don't open this door, I will kick it in. One way or the other we are coming in to get the child." The grandmother replied once again, "I am not opening the door. The child will be staying here tonight." Sergeant Jorgensen raised his right foot and boomed against the door, but because he was standing too close to the door, his leg didn't get fully extended, and the recoil sent him backward and nearly off the porch. I said, "Sergeant, let me give it a try." I put my boot to the door, and not only did the door come open, but I busted the door frame, and the door jammed. "Damn Grimes," one of the other officers yelled, "You have created one hell of a mess."

The child was turned over to the mother and grandma was advised that someone from the city's maintenance department would be out during day hours to repair the door.

It didn't take long for the story to spread around the station about how I destroyed that door, and whenever a supervisor wanted a door kicked open, my services were requested. A few months and four doors later, I came to roll call, and one of the Sergeants presented me with a trophy designed like a boot. It was inscribed "The Key to the City."

Chapter 11
Officer White Only

As the hours of the day slowly dragged by, our next call was a "Neighbor Trouble" call. We arrived on location expecting to see what you normally find on this type of call, people out in front of their houses arguing about something, which is not the case here. We exited our patrol car, and I went up and knocked on the door. My partner walked around back to see if anything was going on back there. The door opened and an elderly white female appeared. Her first words were, "Why are you here? I need a white officer." I advised her that I would be more than happy to address her police needs. She sighed and said, "The little nigger kids that live next door are playing basketball in the street and I want them to stop. Are you going to make them stop or do you think its okay for nigger kids to play in the street?" WOW!!! I took a deep breath and replied, "Ma'am, it is generally not a safe practice for any kid to play in the street no matter what derogatory name or title you place on them, but as far as I can see there are no kids playing in the street anywhere on the block." "They have not been out there at all this week but I am sure they will be back out there soon," she said. As I maintained my professional demeanor with this clearly racist woman, I asked if the kids had damaged any of her property while playing or if they had been loud and disorderly. "No," she replies. Finally, I advised her that no crimes are currently being committed, and she is not providing information of a crime occurring in the past, so there is nothing for me to do at this time.

"I knew it. That was why I wanted the white officer to come." "Okay Ma'am, if you want white, I will get him." I walked off the porch and advised my partner that she was requesting the white officer, so he needed to go and talk to her. Officer White just happened to be a black man with very dark skin. When he told the elderly lady that he was Officer White, she said, "Never mind!" and shut the door. CASE CLOSED!

Chapter 12
Blue Hat And Pink Shirt

The summer days are long and hot in the motor city, and there is no shortage of crime. Unfortunately, way too many calls for police service are not matters for the police, leaving many serious issues on hold and creating slow police response time. That was not the case on this hot July afternoon. It was around 6:30 pm, and the police radio was going nonstop! Every type of call for service was coming over the air.

My partner and I were just ready to clear from a stolen car report when the dispatcher came over the air. "Any car available for 5796 McClellan? We have reports of a black male approximately six feet, one hundred eighty pounds, dark complexion, wearing a blue hat and pink shirt. He is in front of that location assaulting a female and he has a gun in his waistband. ANY UNIT AVAILABLE?"

"Holy shit! We are right around the corner from that location, partner." Five seconds later, we were turning the corner, and sure as shit, we saw a guy matching the description. He was leaning over inside the trunk of a car as we pulled up. I am out of the scout car in a flash with my gun drawn. I yell, "Put your fucking hands up and step back away from the car." Moments later, my partner was out of the car with the shotgun and I heard him rack one in the chamber. The guy turned around, looked at us and said, "Fuck yawl, I am going in the house." He began walking towards the steps; I positioned myself between him and the front porch and again yelled, "Keep your hands where I can see them and walk back and put your hands on the roof of the car."

I advised him that we were there to investigate a report of someone matching his description who was possibly armed. At this point, my partner positioned himself off to the subject's left side and was aimed in. The guy stopped walking but refused to comply with my directions and said, "I've been through all this shit in Nam. I am not afraid of you. If you put that gun down, I will kick your ass." I could see that he had no weapons in his hands, nor did it appear that he had anything in his waistband, so I holstered my weapon and moved in to physically engage him. He took a few steps towards me as if he was ready to fight, and with one quick punch to his right eye, he was on the ground bleeding and crying like a baby and yelling, "You didn't have to do that!"

Quickly, I dropped down on him, placed him on his stomach, and began pulling his hands behind him, attempting to get him cuffed. The struggle was on. I was trying to get his hands behind him, and he was trying to hold them up to his bleeding face. Unfortunately, my partner was not able to assist. He still had the shotgun in his hand and dared not lay it down. The crowd had grown to about 50 people, and on top of that, the woman that this guy had been assaulting (his girlfriend) was now yelling, "Stop hitting him and get off of him." My partner was keeping her at bay as well as watching to make sure no one else tried to intervene. I heard my partner call over his radio for another car to assist; meanwhile, I continued to struggle to get this guy handcuffed.

A few moments later, another police car pulled up and there was another blue uniform on the ground, helping me get the cuffs on this guy. As it turned out, the other uniform was our Sergeant. "Thanks boss," I said with a winded voice, standing up and trying to catch my breath. The Sergeant asked, "Did you find the gun?" "No," my partner replied. "This went from zero to a hundred almost as soon as we got out of the car." "Okay, let's get him in the scout car and try and figure out what was going on here."

The woman who had been yelling at me took off running at some point once the second police car had arrived. I told the Sergeant that when we turned the corner, we saw the subject leaning inside the trunk of the black Ford Mustang parked in front of this location, and when he saw us, he closed the trunk and attempted to go inside the house. That was when I physically detained him.

At this point, we couldn't search the car. We never physically saw a weapon, and to do so, we would need a warrant; nor did we have a complainant to confirm an assault had taken place; none of the bystanders gave any information as to what they witnessed. The only thing we could arrest this asshole for was interfering with an officer investigating a possible felony and resisting arrest. "Okay," the Sergeant says, "let's head to the station before someone else says or does something stupid and we are rolling in the ground again."

Once we got this guy in the station, we processed him and shipped him off to the hospital to get his face stitched up. I cleaned up a little, and we were ready to hit the streets again when the Lieutenant called me to come back to his office.

"What's up Lieutenant?" I asked as I walked through his office door. "Take a seat Grimes." I was thinking that's usually not good when he says that, but I can't think of anything I have done wrong, so I am very interested to see what this conversation will be about.

He starts with, "Grimes. I know you are a good officer." "Thanks Lieutenant," I reply." But while you and your partner were doing your paperwork, a lady came in and made a complaint against you." Almost laughing, I said, "A complaint??? A complaint about what?" "It seems that based on this woman's account of things, after you hit her boyfriend in the face with your nightstick and cut his face open and once you put the handcuffs on him, you then hit her across the back with your stick and that's why she ran away. Furthermore, she has a black and blue bruise on her back to prove it." The Lieutenant continues to tell me that she indeed has a bruise on her back and pictures were taken as possible evidence. "Grimes, before you say anything I have to advise you that you can have a union rep in here with you because I have to file the initial complaint report. Anything you say to me will be entered into my report, or you can say nothing at all and let the investigation take its course."

For the next ten to fifteen seconds, I just sat there analyzing what the fuck I just heard the Lieutenant say. Finally, the first words out of my mouth were, "You got to be fucking kidding me. I don't need a union rep. She is telling a bald-faced lie. No way would I hit someone and not lock them up, besides I never even got a look at this woman. All of my attention was focused on the asshole we arrested. I could hear a female yelling but I couldn't tell you anything about her. And if things happened as she claims they did, that means I assaulted her after me and the Sergeant got him handcuffed. That means I just whacked a woman with my nightstick in the presence of my supervisor and just let her walk away. What the fuck!!!"

"Calm down Grimes. I am just advising you of the complaint. I didn't say I believed it but I still have to file the report. Internal Affairs will have to investigate the complaint." "This is horse shit," I interrupted; "I have to go see Internal Affairs about this?" "Yes, this is standard policy, but you know that Grimes, don't get bent out of shape over this. I am sure it will take care of itself." "I know you are right, Lieutenant, but this is still horse shit."

Chapter 13
I Am Not Crazy

Back on the day shift, the so-called easy shift where we spend most of the morning mopping up calls for service that have gone stale from the night before. The shame of it is that many of these calls needed immediate police response, not an officer knocking at their door five or six hours after the fact asking how they could be of service. I have been cursed out many times by angry citizens and when I tried to explain that we were just dispatched less than 10 minutes ago, even though they dialed 911 at some point in the middle of the night, we were still the ones that had to listen to why the police are the reason the city was going to hell.

Monday mornings were not so bad. I guess people still had a little respect for Sundays. We started this day off with an opportunity to grab a quick breakfast, and then off we went to patrol our area. One of the nice things about the day shift is that officers have a chance to make time to interact with the community to try to build a positive relationship with the citizens. Most officers understood how important building a partnership with the community could make our job easier, but of course, there are too many officers who think that the gun and badge are the means to keep the citizens under control, us against them mentality.

Officer White and I decided to park the car and walk a few of the streets in our sector, shake a few hands, and just mingle a little with the folks. It wasn't long before we came across two seniors playing horseshoes in a vacant lot. As we walked over to engage them in conversation, we heard one say to the other as his horseshoe was in mid flight, "That's a ringer! You can count it."

Sure enough, the shoe hit the stake on the fly making a ringing sound and fell to the ground tightly against the stake. "What did I tell you?" as he slapped his hand against his thigh. "Nice toss," I interjected as we walked up. "Thanks," the younger, heavyset gentleman said as he laughed. "That's the winning shot. Three games in a row. He's no match for me," and he burst out into a full laugh.

The other gentleman, a much smaller man, moaned and said, "I can't do anything with him. His game is sharp! Would one of you young whippersnappers like to give it a go?" White stepped right up. "Sure, I think I can give you a run for your money." The old man laughs again. "Come on sonny, you go first." It didn't take long, game over 21-3. This old guy was good. More laughing, "How about you sonny," referring to me, "Would you like to try your luck?" Laughing, my reply was, "No sir, I clearly see that I am no match for you."

The conversation quickly changed. "What are you officers up to, who are you looking for?" "No one sir," I responded. "We are just out walking, hoping to do just what we are doing, have some good positive interaction with citizens, let you get to know a little about the men and women that serve in your neighborhood." "WOW!" says the smaller gentleman. "Are you planning on running for Mayor or something?" More laughs. "No sir, we just think it is important to get to know as many citizens and have you know a little about who we are underneath these uniforms." I introduced myself, and my partner followed suit. The heavyset gentleman's name was Mr. Cartwright, and the other gentleman was Mr. Evans. "Pleasure meeting you officers," he said with a look of pride and a big smile on his face. Mr. Evans chimed in as we started walking away, "We need more officers like you guys on the force. Be careful and stay safe out here."

We walked for about 15 more minutes; over the prep radio, we received a call for service. "9178 French road. Meet the lady out front of that location; her husband is inside tearing up the house." We hustled back to our patrol car and, in a short time, pulled up to the location. A lady wearing a bathrobe was standing outside. "What is your name and what seems to be the problem?" my partner asked. The lady instantly started crying, "My name is Tonya Wilson and my husband is Larry. I don't know what triggered these actions. He is in there breaking up everything. I didn't know what to do." I asked if there were any weapons in the house. She replied, "No. No guns or anything like that." "Okay, have a seat in our car and we will go in and try to talk with him and figure this out."

I started through the front door with White closely behind me. Once inside, we couldn't hear any movement or any sign of Mr. Larry Wilson. The living room and dining room were both in shambles, with broken furniture and dishes everywhere. "Mr. Wilson," I yelled out, hoping for a response to somewhat identify his location, but nothing.

"This is not going to be easy," I told my partner. "Let's get another unit over here before we go any further." Less than five minutes later, a second crew arrived, and we briefed them before starting a room-by-room search for Mr. Wilson. The main level had been cleared, now the upstairs. There were signs of Mr. Wilson's total destruction of every item in each room. "Damn," one of the other officers commented. "This guy must be pretty pissed off; he has destroyed everything. The only place he can be if he didn't leave out the back door before, we arrived is in the basement." I took the lead and one by one, we made our way into the basement. Although it was ten-thirty in the morning, there was no daylight coming through the windows because of the blinds covering them. The light bulbs were all broken out, so the only light was coming from our flashlights.

"Mr. Wilson, come on out!" I yelled, but not in a threatening tone. The last thing I wanted was for him to pop out from the darkness and attack us. Still no response from him. The basement was in worse shape than the upstairs; there was stuff everywhere. I made my way halfway through the basement and came across a bed mattress leaning against the wall. As I pulled it away, all I could see was two eyes staring at me. I jumped back and yelled, "Oh shit!" Quickly, the other officers were beside me and all flashlights were pointed at him. Mr. Wilson was totally naked, just standing there. We talked him down onto the floor and placed handcuffs on him, mainly for our safety at this point.

Once we had Mr. Wilson upstairs and got him covered, we tried to get him to explain what the hell was going on with him. He didn't speak a word. We had Mrs. Wilson come inside to talk with him, and still nothing. I advised Mrs. Wilson that due to her husband's behavior and her statement of him destroying the house, we were going to transport him to the hospital for a psychiatric evaluation. Mr. Wilson began to curse, kicking his feet and spitting at all of us. Clearly, the thought of going to the hospital was something he was against. Before leaving the scene, I got the Polaroid camera from the patrol car and took several pictures of the condition of the house.

Once we had him in the back seat of our car and headed to the hospital, Mr. Wilson calmly said, "Excuse me officers may I say something?" Shocked, White and I looked at one another. "Yes, what's on your mind?" I replied. "I am not crazy," he said in a normal tone. "I had to act as if I had lost my mind and snapped." "Really?" was my response to this statement. "Why would you need to act as if you are crazy?" Mr. Wilson explained that he had lost his job more than three months ago but had not told his wife; all the money had run out and he had no other recourse. He continued to say he felt the only way he could get some assistance for his wife and three kids was to be committed to the crazy house, paving the way for Mrs. Wilson to be eligible for state assistance.

It was clear to us that he was not crazy but desperate. We told him there were other ways to get financial help. He interrupted, saying, "I have tried everything. There are no other options. I have to act crazy and get put away so my family can survive, end of story."

We were now only a few minutes away from the hospital. Mr. Wilson said, "You guys are ok with me. You didn't manhandle me or beat me down, like I am sure other officers would have done, and I thank you. When we get inside the hospital, I am going to act a complete fool just so you guys know. Let the orderlies handle me. I don't want to do anything where you guys might get hurt."

Once inside the hospital, Mr. Wilson didn't disappoint us; his performance was Oscar-worthy. My partner and I went into the office, filled out the necessary forms for comment, attached the pictures from the house, and headed back through the hospital to our car. I looked in the holding area where Mr. Wilson was now being held. We made eye contact. He winked and nodded his head as if to say thank you.

Chapter 14
Keep Your Hat On

"Hey partner, happy anniversary." Yep, three years on the job and it was everything I hoped it to be. We were on the afternoon shift again, and one thing for sure was that there would be no dull moments this evening. We are 43 service calls behind. As we roll out of the station's parking lot, my partner says, "Let's go make this city safe!" First call up, meet the manager at the market at Fairview and Kercheval for an adult male shoplifter. We walked inside the store and the manager was holding the subject at gunpoint. "Hey sir, put the gun away now!" White yelled. The suspect, sensing we may be on his side, started screaming at the manager, "You had no right to pull that gun on me. I was going to pay for that shit." "Pipe down sir, and stand up. I need to pat you down. Do you have anything on you that may stick me or harm me? Tell me now because if I stick myself checking you, you are really going to have a bad day."

"Officers, please look at my surveillance video. You can see this guy was attempting to steal my merchandise." Ten seconds after viewing the video, the handcuffs went on; this guy had stuffed several items inside his shirt. It was a quick felony arrest and we are back on the street.

The first few hours into the shift had gone pretty quickly. "How about lunch," I asked my partner before it gets crazy out here." "Sounds good. Let's do it," Officer White replied, laughing. We decided on Italian food and pulled into a popular dining spot, and not to our surprise; there were two other police cars already in the lot.

We placed our orders and the food had just hit the table when the prep radio screamed, "Officer down! Officer down!" "Damn, damn, damn," as we and four other officers jumped up from our tables like a synchronized swim team racing towards the door. Again, the radio screamed, "Officer down! Officer down! We need help!" This time, their location follows the screams. "Shit! They are in the projects," one of the other officers yelled as he was getting into his car.

We were about two and a half miles away; flashing lights and sirens were blaring as we pulled out onto Mack Avenue and headed westbound. Two minutes later, we were in the parking lot of the projects, and officers were running everywhere, looking for the officers needing help. Finally, we heard, "They're over here." There are probably a hundred officers at the scene by now. Two officers from the narcotics unit were attempting to make a buy and their cover was blown. Both officers were hit several times, but thank God both are still conscious and alert. The shitheads that shot them had gotten away.

Two EMS rigs rolled in at the same time, and the wounded officers were loaded and en route to the hospital with several police cars escorting them. Here at the scene, the search is on. "No one goes in or out of this motherfucker," yelled a plainclothes officer. He turned out to be the wounded officers' Lieutenant.

We spent the next couple of hours in the projects, shaking down everything that moved; unfortunately, we came up dry. The word came over the radio that both officers were going to make it. That's great news, and the anger and tension in the air came down several notches.

The anger hit the ceiling again as White and I made it back to our police car, and we were approached by a plainclothes officer identifying himself as a Sergeant from the Professional Standards Unit. Of all things, he asked, "Officers, where are your hats?" "Really," I replied, "you are asking about us not having our hats on at the scene where not one but two officers have been shot? Respectfully sir! You have got to be fucking kidding me!" It seemed that this asshole Sergeant didn't use any discretion when it came to department policies and procedures. He wrote up every officer at the scene who didn't have their hats on; ties clipped on properly, shirt sleeves not buttoned, and anything else he could find.

You couldn't imagine the grief the Lieutenant was hearing at off-duty roll call. Every officer on our shift received a write-up at the shooting scene, and the officers were letting management have it. There even were talks of a sick out. That was a little extreme, in my opinion, but others were serious. The Lieutenant listened calmly to all of the bitching, then finally said, "Guys, don't worry about the write ups. The paperwork will be sent to me for processing and disciplinary action. I will take care of everything; no one will see them make it into their file." The Lieutenant's last words on the matter were, "Be mindful that the Professional Standards Unit has personnel out there monitoring your activities, so act accordingly, hats on, ties clipped on when you get out of your cars."

Things seem to have settled down over the last week since the officers were shot. Calls for service were pretty basic, if there was ever such a thing. It was almost as if the bad guys knew we needed a break from the craziness when an officer was shot.

I looked at my watch and said to my partner, "Wow! This day has gone by fast. Only one more hour until the end of our shift." Over the radio, "Any car available? 6182 Seminole, an elderly woman is reporting someone is breaking into her house." I grabbed the mic. "Dispatch scout 5-8 is right around the corner. Show us handling that call." Officer White ripped the patrol left onto Seminole Street, and five houses down, we were there. We jumped out and ran into the front yard. I told him I was headed around back.

As I turned the corner at the rear of the house, I could see the silhouette of a person pushing his shoulder against the door. "Freeze motherfucker or you are dead." "Please, please don't shoot me," the male voice screamed. "I live here with my grandmother." "Get on the ground," I ordered the slender black male. He willingly complied. My partner was in the front, investigating the area and he came running around the corner, "Are you okay partner?" he asked. "Yep. I'm good." A check of his identification confirmed the young man was telling the truth. He had lost his keys and knew his grandmother would never come to the door at that time of night if he had knocked. We were able to have the 911 operator advise the elderly caller that the police were there and advised her it was okay to come open the door.

Just when we thought we had a happy ending to another tour of duty and were about to get back into our patrol car, who pulled up in an unmarked police car? "Yep." That damn Sergeant from the Professional Standards Unit. "Officers, where are your hats?" I was ready to lose it, but nope, screw it if this guy felt the need to write us up, the hell with it. He didn't disappoint me.

Chapter 15
Wrong Way Crash

Time is flying; summer has ended and fall was a blur. Snow and ice are now the normal weather conditions. Not an hour into the shift, over the air, came a unit, "We are chasing a blue Ford westbound on Warren from St. Jean, possibly a stolen vehicle." "Hey partner, they are about a mile away but coming our way. Let's get in position in case they make it this far down." I accelerated down the side street to the corner and made a left onto Charlevoix which had me going the wrong way on a one-way street. Quickly, another left turn at the next side street and we were now headed towards Warren. The chase was continuing in our direction, westbound on Warren.

Sure enough, here they came, blasting past us. I fell in behind the police crew in pursuit. We were now the secondary unit. My partner advised dispatch that we were the secondary unit so that all other units coming to assist would know to parallel the chase. This guy clearly didn't want to go to jail today; he was driving at speeds close to 100 miles per hour. I was thinking this is not going to end well, and maybe the primary unit should break off the chase. It was five-fifteen pm; the rush hour was in full effect and we were crossing Van Dyke Avenue. Damn! We just went airborne. A few blocks later, the bad guy attempted to make a right turn onto a residential street. Bad idea, as he wiped out several parked cars. By the time we turned the corner, the primary officers were out of the patrol car chasing this guy between the houses. Officer White jumped out of our vehicle to secure the scene and make sure no one was injured in the crash. I accelerated down the street to the next corner and made a left turn, attempting to get a couple of blocks ahead of the suspect.

Three blocks down, I turned left and headed toward the end of the block, hoping this guy would run right into me. I meant that figuratively, but he literally ran from between the houses and right across in front of me. Oh shit. I hit the brake and ripped the steering wheel to the right, striking a parked car. I jumped out in close pursuit. The original two officers were losing ground fast. Damn! This guy should have been on a track team; not only was he fast, but he also had endurance. I was not letting this asshole get away. I had crashed my patrol car and that meant a shit load of paperwork for me.

We went into another backyard and over a fence, and just as I was getting winded and the suspect was ready to jump another fence, he stopped cold. A Pit bull dog was awaiting his arrival. The suspect fell to the ground and said, "Fuck it. I give up." I jumped on top of him and put my gun to his head. "Don't move! I am too tired to fight with you, so I will just shoot your ass." The other two officers finally arrived and we handcuffed him.

I arrived back at my patrol car to the waiting owner of the vehicle I hit; he was visibly upset with me but was understanding. I advised him of what steps to take to have his car repaired. As for my patrol car, the damage was very minor. Thank goodness for the push bumper on the front. Our Sergeant arrived on the scene and was not happy because he had three times the paperwork. He had to do the investigation for the chase, a second investigation and recommendation on the initial crash, and finally, an investigation and recommendation on my accident. I truly saw what the Lieutenant meant when he said, "Once you make Sergeant, you had better study your ass off to make Lieutenant. Sergeants are the hardest workers in the department." Nevertheless, my paperwork still took the rest of the shift to complete.

Chapter 16
A Near Tragic Mistake

It's January, and we are on the afternoon shift. Roll call is over, and it's time to hit the streets. The snow was coming down hard; my partner said, "What do you want to do today, drive in this mess or jump and have to write all the reports for the accidents I am sure we will be responding to this evening?" With a groan, I said, "I will drive and you can have the reports."

The police radio was quiet for most of the shift. I guess people were staying home off the streets. "Ten o'clock," Officer White said. "This day is almost over." We were both looking forward to the next three weeks to pass because we both were going on vacation.

A few minutes later, dispatch was calling us for an attempted rape that just happened. We were not very far from the location and arrived in about four minutes. Once inside the house, a young lady about 25 years old was sitting on the couch with her mother and father on each side, trying to console her. The young lady was crying uncontrollably and with good reason. After a few minutes of talking with her and her parents, we were able to get some information about what happened.

The young lady had arrived home and, as usual, pulled down the alley to park her car in the garage. Tonight would be different. After parking the vehicle and getting out to close the garage door, someone grabbed her from behind and took her to the ground inside the garage. Through her tears and crying, she told us she felt that she was in the fight of her life as the perpetrator began punching her in the face and pulling at her coat and clothes.

He produced a large knife, placed it to her neck and told her that one more scream and he would leave her dead on the garage floor. She slowly was able to tell us how he made her remove her coat and lay there as he ripped her buttons down, opening her dress and exposing her undergarments. She began crying uncontrollably again, "He was going to rape me. Oh my God!" My blood was boiling on the inside; I felt terrible for what this lady had just endured. In one tug, the rapist snatched off her panties and pulled his penis from his pants when she heard her father call out from the back porch, "Baby girl, is that you out there?" She screamed in a crying voice, "Daddy! Daddy!" "If you had not come out and scared him off, I would still be laying out there raped and probably dead," she said to her dad. "Oh my God! Oh my God!" I have participated in hundreds of interviews of victims, but I have to tell you this one tore at my core.

I let my partner know that I was going out to the garage to check out the scene of the crime and look for possible evidence, and because of the newly fallen snow, see if there was a chance of getting a K-9 here for a track. Her dad walked me through the house to the back door and pointed towards the sidewalk to the door for the garage. Then he turned and went back to his daughter.

This is when my life and the lives of this family nearly suffered a great tragedy. I walked out to the garage, gun drawn, not expecting to find anyone out there but prepared just in case. Just as I approached the garage door entrance, an unknown man stepped out of the garage. In a flash, my gun was up and pointed at his face, and with God as my witness, the only thing that saved this man's life was not through any training I had ever received. I cocked the hammer on my revolver instead of simply pulling the trigger.

"Don't shoot! Don't shoot!" he yelled. "I am her brother. I came out here to see if I could see who did this to my sister." The unexpected surprise of this man stepping out of that garage nearly cost him his life and my career and sanity, I am sure.

I quickly holstered my weapon and, while pointing, yelled, "Get back in the house!" The brother, running at a brisk pace with me closely behind, entered the back door to the house. I locked eyes on the father and before I realized it, I was now screaming at the top of my voice, "Why the hell didn't you tell me your son was out there? I damn near killed him." Now the mother was screaming and crying, "Dear God. I almost lost both of my babies. Oh God! Oh God!" Officer White, with a very calm voice, said, "Okay, everybody try to relax a little. God was with us this evening."

I step outside on the front porch to get a grip. My heart was still pounding like it wanted to jump out of my chest and my hands were shaking uncontrollably. Finally, I was able to call over the radio, requesting a supervisor and a K-9 officer.

A short time later, both units arrived on location and the K-9 was able to track the footprints left in the snow. Unfortunately, the track went cold after a few blocks and the suspect crossed a major street. The K-9 lost the scent. Back at the house, the sergeant tried to convince the young lady to go to the hospital to get checked out just as a precaution, but she refused, stating that the perpetrator's assault did not result in penetration, and her injuries were psychological, not physical.

We cleared the scene and returned to the station to knock out the report. Thank goodness our shift was over by the time my partner completed the paperwork because I was not mentally fit to go back on patrol.

Chapter 17
Letting A Murderer Go Free

Spring is in the air, and Officer White and I have another year under our belt. It's nice to be working the day shift; the radio traffic is much slower, and it's nice to have some easy days out here. Two weeks have passed and it truly has been slow. Trust me, that is not a complaint.

I mentioned to White, "How about we go by the park and see if any of the young fellows are out playing basketball." "Sounds like a plan," he said, "but first, let's get some breakfast in our system." "Roger that," was my quick reply.

The park was bursting with kids out having a ball. The basketball court was in full effect. We got out of the patrol car and I yelled, "The ole school ball players are here and we got next game." That announcement brought a thunderous laugh from the entire court. "Don't you all have some heads to crack open?" came from an agitated voice. Another voice yelled, "The seniors are playing at the YMCA," which brought an even louder laugh. We even had to laugh at that. "What's the problem?" White asked. "You guys afraid of some ole school lessons?" "Okay cool. You guys, I mean you officers of the law, have next game." More laughs from the crowd.

We got off to a quick start, 4-0; the first team to 10 was the winner. Game over. We lost 10-4. "Wow! What happened?" I said to White. "You can't play defense anymore Rod. Your guy scored the last seven points." A voice yelled out, "Hey, Starsky & Hutch, thanks for the lessons. Could that be why our school system is failing?" Now, the crowd was rolling on the ground, laughing. I gave them the thumbs up and a quick wave as we made it back to the patrol car. As we drove off, Officer White got on the loudspeaker and said, "The basketball court is closed. We are sore losers." The crowd laughed again as we drove away. "That went well," White laughed. "Yes, yes it did, even though we didn't let the youngsters win on purpose. It was better that they did, you know, for community morale."

The police dispatch chimed in, "scout 5-8 and any other available units. In the alley rear of 5792 Lemay, three men stripping a vehicle in progress." Officer White answered, "We're on the way," as he flicked on the red and blue overhead lights. Two more units answered to assist. "Wow, 10:30 in the morning and they are stripping a car in daylight," I said to White. "Where's the shame?"

All three units arrived at the same time, and sure as shit, there were the three knuckleheads taking parts off a red Ford and putting them into a black van. We swooped down on them as they scattered in different directions. They gave us a run for our money, but at the end of the day, three running and six chasing was no contest. We had them on the ground and cuffed in just a few minutes.

Back at the station, there was a ton of paperwork to do, so we split it among the three crews. White and I took the black van. We ran a check, and sure enough, it was stolen as well. We inventoried the parts from the red Ford as well as parts from other vehicles which I was sure were stolen. The younger officers took the arrest report and prisoner processing. We figured it would look good on their record of getting credit for nabbing three felons.

A week had passed since the car theft arrest when I happened to see one of the young officers who wrote the arrest report and went to court on the case. "What's going on, crime fighter," I joked with the young officer. "Did the car thieves cop a plea?" The young officer dropped his head and quietly said the case was dismissed. "WHAT!!! What happened?" "The judge released them on a technicality because there were a few things we left out on the arrest report." "Damn!" I replied. That was some good work that had gone down the drain. "No worries," I told the young officer. "Those assholes will screw up again and we will be there to get them; keep your head up."

One month after the judge released Jeffery Simpson and his brothers on a technicality for stealing and stripping the cars, Jeffery broke into the dorm room of a Wayne State University student, thinking the kid was in class, but the kid was home studying. Jeffery took the poor kid to the basement of the building and blew his head off.

This was the second time in my career I wanted to quit. Damn! Some kid lost his life because this asshole was released after being caught dead to rights for stealing and stripping cars. He never should have been out on the street. This senseless loss of life has shaken me to the core.

Six months have passed, and the murdering asshole's trial has started. Even though I was not involved in this case, I felt compelled to attend the trial. I was working the midnight shift, so going to court during the day was not an issue for my schedule. I took a seat in the back of the courtroom, that was filled mostly with people who knew or were related to the victim. The defendant was led into the courtroom by the deputies. Someone screams, "You murdering son of a bitch! I am going to see that you rot in hell." "Order in the court!" as the judge slammed his gavel down. "I will not tolerate that kind of outburst in my courtroom." The same male voice screamed, "He killed my son and he needs to pay with his life." Once again, the judge repeated his orders and the crowd which was reacting to the dad's outburst, began to settle down.

The jury was made up of eight women and four men; seven members were black, three were white, one was Asian, and one was Hispanic. The victim was Middle Eastern and the defendant was black. The judge was a white male. The prosecutor was a white female. Talk about a diverse group.

The prosecutor began with her opening remarks. "I want to tell you about two people. The first person was a young man that grew up here in the city on the north end. He and his family of eight lived in a single-family house with one bathroom and three bedrooms. His father worked 12-to-15-hour days between two jobs to make ends meet. This young man went to school every day and after school he spent hours learning a second language. He graduated high school, not at the top of his class, but he had worked hard enough to earn a scholarship to Wayne State University. He was the second oldest child, and understood his role in the family was to excel in his studies and be an example for his younger brothers and sisters, which he did. I won't tell you his name at this point, but I am sure you will figure it out in short order. One day the young man, 19 years of age, was sitting in his dorm room studying. He was in his room and not in class that day only because he was not feeling well that morning. Even though he was sick, he still pulled out his books to study. After all, he clearly understood his family responsibility and refused to let his sickness deter him from adding to his learning that day."

"Now I want to tell you about a second young man," she continued. "This person also grew up in the city and lived on the lower east side. He and his three brothers were raised by his mother. His dad had been killed years ago while attempting to rob a party store. The young man is also 19 years of age. He, unlike the first gentleman I spoke of, dropped out of school after the eighth grade and turned to street crimes. This individual spent his young teenage years in and out of the juvenile system until he became of age, and then it was jail. He has been arrested for drugs, assault, weapons, and auto theft, who by the way was arrested and released on a technicality a week before the death of the victim in this case."

The prosecutor began to wrap up her opening statement by saying, "These two men are the reason we are here today. Unfortunately, only one of them is here in this courtroom; that's because he committed the murder of the other. Ladies and gentlemen of the jury, we will present evidence to prove this beyond a reasonable doubt that the person sitting at the defendant table committed that murder. I am sure you know by now which young man is of the two I described earlier."

"Objection!" the defense attorney screamed as he jumped out of his seat. "Your honor, this is outrageous. The prosecutor has gone over the line with her remarks. Her acts are so egregious that I am asking your honor to declare a mistrial." The courtroom erupted. "Order! Order!" the judge yelled to no avail. "Clear the courtroom," the judge directs the deputies.

The courtroom was empty in a matter of seconds. I was able to stay because I identified myself as a police officer. The jury was escorted back to their holding room, and I sat and witnessed one of the deepest ass-kicking I had ever seen a prosecutor take. The judge then threatened to hold her in contempt and put her on a very short leash but did not declare a mistrial. The audience and jury were brought back in and the defense attorney gave his opening remarks.

Two and a half weeks and the trial was over. The asshole was found guilty of first-degree murder. I was there for every minute and was glad this guy would be off the streets for the rest of his life, but something in me had changed. I think it's time for me to take a break from patrol work.

Chapter 18
Expired License

Fall is in the air and I am still working in precinct patrol. It is difficult to get a transfer unless you have more than 12 to 15 years in the force. Most of the veteran officers snatch up the assignments in the bureaus. Until something comes along, I will just have to go out there and give it all I have.

Saturday night was bowling night, and it was always a great time with friends. My best friend since 10th grade and I were sitting in the bowling alley bar; we had been reflecting on our career paths. It was funny because shortly after I joined the force, he went down to recruiting and signed up. James is a guy who has always been a few pounds overweight, and it was a sticking point for him coming on the force. He was told that he needed to lose 25 pounds before he could be considered for testing. James would listen to my stories and gruel at the idea of being an officer.

"Let's get down to business James," I said. "If you really want to do this, then I am going to help you lose weight." Our other bowling teammate, Bruce, made the same pledge. "Rod and I will work out with you and in a couple of months we will get that excess weight off you. How about we get started on Monday."

At six o'clock pm sharp, there was a knock at my door; both James and Bruce standing there bright-eyed. The workouts were taking place at my house. I have quite a bit of exercise equipment, along with a video camera to record his progress. "Come on in," and straight to the basement we went. I had already put together a program for James to follow; two hours and a puddle of sweat later, day one was over.

"Damn! You guys didn't tell me you were going to take me to near death to get this done." "You will be ok James," I laughed. "It will get easier each day; we are just waking up those muscles you have not used in a while. You need to prepare yourself for severe soreness in about 36 hours. It will last for about two days; your body is in shock right now."

Three weeks had passed, and James was not losing any weight. This was not making sense. The diet we put him on was only 1400 calories per day. That, along with the workout regiment, should have caused a change.

Bruce walked in a few minutes early for today's session. I noticed that he was not his normal upbeat self today. "What's going on?" I asked. "You seem to be distant." "No, I am good," he replied. "James should be here in a few minutes and we can get started." I knew there was something wrong, but I was not going to pry any further.

Six o'clock pm, right on time, James walked through the door. "Hey guys. How's it going?" he asked with a cheerful smile. "Are we ready to do this?" After the warm-ups and stretching, James was on the weight bench, ready for bench press. Bruce was handling the spot and I was the ra ra man. "Come on James. Fourth set lets go. You can do it, six, seven. Come on James. Push!" I encouraged as he was getting winded. Bruce put both of his hands on the bar and instead of palms under to help, his palms were on top to push downward. James couldn't push anymore. He had no strength. Bruce asked, "So James, what did you do today?" James struggled and replied, "The usual." On Fridays, he would go to the music resale shop. "What did you do after that James?" Bruce asked. I was wondering what the hell was going on; why was Bruce interrogating James while he was in the middle of this set? James said, "I went home and relaxed to get ready for this evening's workout. Come on. Help me. I can't get this bar up."

Bruce showed no mercy. I was totally confused, but I stayed silent. "What did you eat?" he asked James. James hesitated, "Nothing other than what's on my diet plan for today." "Really!" Bruce yelled. "Well, explain what you were doing in the parking lot of the Burger King on Woodward Ave. by the zoo." Now, the weight bar was resting on James's chest and Bruce was pushing down on it. "What? What the hell is he talking about James?" was now my question. "Okay, okay. Get this bar off me and I will tell you everything."

James got up off the weight bench and slowly sat down in a chair against the wall. "What were you doing there?" Bruce snapped again, "And don't lie because I saw you. What did you eat?" James dropped his head; "I had a whopper and fries." "What else James? Spill all the beans." "Well, I had two whoppers; the fries were the large size, an apple pie and ex-large coke." I chimed in with, "So James, do you want us to believe that you had regular whoppers, or were they double meat with cheese?" "Yes, they were double meat with cheese," in a soft voice. "Damn! No wonder you are not losing weight. You are eating everything you have always eaten. What's the point in coming over to work out?" To make matters worse, I stopped by James' house a few days later and learned from his mother that James raids the refrigerator every night after everyone has gone to bed. Needless to say, Bruce and I discontinued the workouts. Months later, James got a job at the post office. His dad has been in management for several years, so I am sure that helped with his hiring.

James was going to pay a penalty for having us put in all of this time when he was not really serious. What can I do to get back at him? That's when it hit me. His birthday was coming up in a few days and I knew he had not renewed his driver's license and tabs yet. Monday morning after roll call, I told my partner that I had a prank and needed to play on a good friend. I explained everything to my partner and he was totally down for helping me get some payback.

We left the station and headed over to the area of James' new apartment building. I told my partner we would sit here and do traffic enforcement for a while and wait for James to leave his building. 10:45 am, we saw James' car pull off the side street onto Woodward Avenue. "That's him partner." The plan was for us to make a traffic stop. My partner would go to the driver's side and I would stand off to the right out of sight.

James is a very safe driver and usually obeys all the traffic laws, so for him to see a police car in his rearview mirror would put him on edge. We pulled in behind his vehicle as he cruised northbound up Woodward. After about a half mile, I activated the red and blue emergency lights and hit the siren. I saw James' reaction as he appeared a little shocked that he was being pulled over. Without hesitation, he safely pulled his car to the curb. Quickly, I jumped out and took my position out of his view. Moments later, my partner walked slowly up to the driver's door, and in his most official and professional voice, Officer Donaldson said "License, registration and proof of insurance please." James, totally unaware as to what was going on, replied, "Yes sir, but can you tell me what did I do wrong?" Instantly, my partner yelled, "Oh, you are going to be a smart ass uh? Just give me the fucking paperwork or I'm going to haul your ass off to jail. Now shut the fuck up." There was silence coming from inside the vehicle, and moments later, James produced the paperwork. "What's this shit?" my partner barked at James. "This registration has expired, and so is your drivers license. Give me your updated paperwork asshole." Wow! My partner was really giving it to James; I was almost starting to feel bad for him. James started to explain that his birthday was yesterday which was Sunday and he did not get to the Secretary of State office on Friday. "Oh, so you are just going to drive around dirty huh?" James began to explain, "Sir, I am on my way to the Secretary of State's office now to renew them." "You think I just got out of the academy this morning, and I am going to fall for that bullshit lie?" Officer Donaldson was piling it on thick.

"You are in violation. I am going to impound your car and you are going to jail." "What? Wait," James screamed in a frightened voice. "Do you really have to do this?" Officer Donaldson asked James, "What do you mean? Are you asking if I can look the other way on this?" "Yes," replied James with a very submissive voice. "What's in it for me if I let you go?" My partner asked. James stepped into it deeper when he said, "I only have an extra $20 dollar bill on me." "Get your ass out of the car," my partner yelled. "You are trying to bribe me with money. Now I know I am taking you to jail." I was really starting to enjoy this shit now and it was difficult for me not to bust out laughing. James asked my partner, "Do you know Officer Grimes? He's my best friend. He can vouch for me. I am not a bad person." "Yes, I know Officer Grimes. I think he is the biggest asshole in the department. So, if that's the name you are going to drop you are shit out of luck! You would have been better off saying let me take you to Burger King and offer to buy me two double meat whoppers with cheese, a large fry, an apple pie and a coke. That might have gotten you off the hook."

I couldn’t take it anymore. I burst out laughing. James looked over to the right side of the car to see me leaning against the building, crying and laughing. Now Officer Donaldson was busting a gut laughing. The look on James' face was priceless as he began to catch his breath from near hyperventilation. Now we were all laughing. “This is payback for the wasted training you did for the academy.” James admitted this was really a good trick. “Okay, you are one up Rod.” “Let’s go partner. My work here is done,” laughing as we walked back to the patrol car.

The rest of the day was slow and easy, so we racked up our numbers on traffic tickets. Donaldson has turned out to be a pretty good partner since we have been together; I still kind of miss White, though.

Chapter 19
A Terrible Day For Detroit Police Department

Another day in the city with the temperature north of 90 degrees. The streets were jumping, and calls for service were coming over the police radio one after another. The dispatch had us respond to NBD on W. Seven Mile Road, a possible hold-up in progress. We were several miles away, so my partner hit the lights and siren as I maneuvered the car into the left turn lane and headed westbound. There's one good thing about Detroit drivers. For the most part, when they hear or see an emergency vehicle coming, they will move to the side of the road. About a half mile away, the siren went off and we were running just the lights. "Watch out!" my partner yelled. "That guy is not stopping." I had already anticipated how to get around the gray pickup headed northbound on Wyoming Street. "Wow, good driving partner," Donaldson whimpered out. "Thanks. I got this." Seconds later, we were in front of the bank. We sat observing for a few moments and noticed that people were coming and going in a very normal fashion. We entered the bank casually; everything appeared normal. I separated from my partner and found the manager. "Everything okay, sir?" I asked. "Yes," he replied with a surprised look. At that moment, one of the tellers came up. "I'm sorry sir," she said to the manager. "I accidentally pushed the alarm button at my window. I was afraid to come tell you but when I saw the police come in, I figured I had better come let you know."

The manager was instantly heated, "Don't you know the protocols Ms. Whitfield?" He then turned back to me, "I am so sorry for this, Officer. I will deal with this matter." "Sure thing sir. We will get out of here if there is nothing you need from us."

Back in the car, and just as we pulled away from the bank, over the air came the alert that a citywide notification was about to be broadcast. As officers, we always hold our breath in hopes it was not an officer-down notification. Sure, as shit, "All units, all units. We have officers down in the 13th district." "Three officers shot." Fuck, fuck, fuck," my partner was yelling. "Calm down and make sure you are getting the address correct," I responded. We are at least 10 miles away. No need to go to the location. Let's just get in position to block traffic on the route being used to get them to the hospital."

We notified dispatch that we would post at John R and Grand Blvd which was about two miles from the hospital. We arrived and quickly shut down all traffic. The intersection was clear and all traffic was forced to sit at the curb until we released them. I was handling the vehicles on John R. I walked to each driver, letting them know that this was now an emergency route and several police cars and EMS wagons would be passing through at a very high speed. I asked them to please stay in their cars and, by all means, not to move their vehicle.

It seemed like forever, but only a few minutes had passed when I began to hear the sirens and then saw the lights. Ten or 12 police cars leading with 2 EMS wagons closely behind, followed by not less than 25 more police cars. The route was completely blocked so the escort could roll without fear of any unsuspecting traffic. They were taking full advantage; their speeds were probably over one hundred miles per hour.

Once they cleared our intersection, we released the traffic and headed to the hospital. We couldn't get within three blocks because there were so many police vehicles parked everywhere. As we were walking up, other officers were passing by us, many crying uncontrollably. Damn! This was not a good sign. We knew that the possibility of being injured in the line of duty could happen at any time. What was still difficult to handle was when an officer was shot, or worse, shot and killed. The reactions we were seeing led me to believe the latter. We made our way into the emergency entrance of the hospital. There were officers everywhere crying and sobbing. That's when I heard a Lieutenant talking on the phone. "Yes sir. We have lost two of the three and the last one was rushed into surgery. I will keep you posted sir." Then he hung up. "Lieutenant, sir. I wasn't eavesdropping on your conversation but I couldn't help but overhear part of what you were saying." He interrupted me, "No worries, Officer. We are all family and this has cut the family deeply." I went on to ask, "Would it be out of line for me to ask what happened that we now have two dead officers, and a third in surgery fighting for his life?" The Lieutenant paused for a moment, then said, "I can only share this. What happened today will surely change the way we do things in this department. You will have to wait until the Chief releases the official details relating to this tragic event."

Something big like this, I knew I wouldn't have to wait for the Chief to make a formal announcement. Surely, there were officers already talking about it. I walked back outside. There were even more officers filling the walkway and street than when I had arrived only five minutes ago. The early chatter was narcotic officers were raiding a house and they were ambushed by the drug dealers. That quickly changed to rookie uniform patrol officers were trying to do an unauthorized narcotic raid on a well-known dope dealer, and things went south.

I walked through the sea of blue uniforms, looking for my partner and anyone that I knew working in the 13th district. Across the way, I spotted Officer Randy Hawkins, the "HAWK," as we affectionately called him; he was assigned to the 13th district. He was standing against the building, crying almost uncontrollably. I walked over and said, "Hey man. That's right, just let it go." I gave him a long hug, not letting go until I felt him ready to be released. "There's no shame. Get it out." A few minutes passed, and he began to regain his composure. "Thanks man," he said softly. I replied, "We always have to be here for one another. I am glad I could be here for you." He began to talk about how bad the scene looked when he arrived. I said, "Oh, you were at the scene Hawk?" "Yes, and it was terrible."

"I was only a block away when the shooting started," he said. "I could hear the gunshots. It sounded like a small war. The last of the shots ended as I came to a screeching stop six houses from the location. Then the screams of 'Officer down! Officer down! 112 Woodlawn, officers down". Hawk went on to tell me the gist of what had happened.

Apparently, one uniform patrol unit had been dispatched to the location to investigate several men possibly armed with guns. Just the day before, someone had been shot at that house. It was known to be a dope house, so a second unit was dispatched to assist. Hawk said he and his partner decided to head that way just for moral support due to the nature of the call and the recent history. Unknowingly to the patrol officers or the zone dispatcher, the Narcotic Section had scheduled a raid on the house today. While the uniform officers were inside shaking down the occupants, the plainclothes narcotic officers hit the door and made entry, unaware the uniform officers were inside conducting a separate investigation about possible armed individuals at the location. As you can see, this was a situation about to go bad. The plainclothes officers ran in yelling, "POLICE, POLICE" with their guns drawn. The uniform officers inside saw unidentified men running in with guns. The first narcotic officer was taken for a bad guy by one of the uniform officers and was shot twice. The remaining narcotic team continued to make entry, knowing they were meeting gunfire, and began shooting everything that moved. One uniform officer attempted to get away from the gunfire and dove out the front window onto the porch. He was shot by one of the narcotic officers before he realized he was shooting at a uniformed police officer. "What a fucking cluster fuck." Then Hawk broke down crying again.

A couple of days passed, and the Chief presented to the department and to the public the details of that sad day which included an early report on the status of a third officer who was recovering after surgery. It seems that a call came into the 911 emergency center stating that the person responsible for the shooting at that location the day before was seen leaving the location early that morning. The information given by the 911 operator to the dispatcher was drastically different than that given to the officers responding. Which was "Several men at the location armed with guns," that was the first error.

Because the narcotics section was having a problem with targets being tipped off, the department had a policy that the narcotics section would not notify any other department personnel to be made aware of their movement. This policy made sense on paper, but clearly, Monday morning quarterbacking said differently. Having plain clothes officers with no identifying marking on their person or vehicles and with many of them looking like what a typical drug user would look like, along with the fact that they have various types of guns on them, puts the uniformed officer in a very bad position.

The next major mistake made was the Narcotic Raid Team did not pay any attention to the two marked police cars parked in close proximity to the house they were raiding or where those officers may have been when they executed the raid. When you put all that together, it's amazing that we have not had similar incidents before now. Two narcotic officers were shot, one dead and one uniform officer dead. A police officer's funeral is a very tragic thing, but to have two to attend in three days can take a toll on the most hardened officer.

A police officer's funeral is very difficult!

The Lieutenant I had spoken with at the hospital was correct. This event changed the way our department conducted its narcotic raids, as well as how information received by the 911 operator was communicated and passed on to the dispatcher.

Chapter 20
Dealership Homicide

The calendar said fall, but today, the temperature was still warm. This summer had been a blur, but the pain and hurt of losing two officers was fresh.

I had a new regular partner, Jeffery Sotherland, another academy classmate. Jeff was a quiet and reserved officer, but didn't take his quietness for weakness. He was a third-degree black belt in martial arts, and also did some boxing in the army. "Hey Jeff, guess who's driving today." "Sure Rod, I will grip it today." We rolled off the ramp and headed for the Dairy Queen to get a cold drink. It was a typical warm, sunny September afternoon. Wow! It looked like all of the neighborhood kids were there to get a cold treat.

We got out of the patrol car and walked up to the rear of the line, ready to wait our turn. Suddenly, we heard the adult voice coming from inside the Dairy Queen window. "Officers, come on up. What can I get for you guys?" Quickly came loud objections from a couple of the kids. "How are you just going to wait on them before helping us? That's not fair! We are spending our money and I bet you will probably give them theirs for free." I started telling the owner that we were okay with waiting our turn when Officer Sotherland interrupted me. "Thank you, sir, for getting us served quickly."

I immediately began to wonder if Jeff and I were going to make a good team. I was not big on using the badge to get special treatment. Jeff ordered a strawberry milkshake, then turned and asked me what I was having. Quickly I responded, "I will take a lemonade slush." "Sure thing," the owner replied, and sarcastically said, "It's on the house officers." Boy, this whole scene was not playing out very well in building a trustful, fair partnership with our young citizens in the community. The voice rose as he addressed the group of about fifteen kids, mostly boys, "These officers come to work every day and put their lives on the line for us citizens, which includes you young guys; oh, and young ladies. Yes, I will serve them first so they can be back out there looking out for our safety and best interest." Our order was up in no time, and the owner said, "See you guys were only delayed about one minute," and then began to take the first young man's order.

I turned and began walking back to the patrol car but could feel that my partner was not walking with me. I turned around, and sure enough, Jeff was just standing there sipping on his milk shake. "What is he doing?" I was thinking. "Is he trying to rub it in the kids' faces?" "Sotherland," I called out. "Let's roll." He put his finger in the air, indicating he wanted me to wait. We stood there until every kid had placed their order, and this was when I knew I had a great guy for a partner. Strickland told the owner, "You have to give all these kids their order free just as you did us. But surely you are not in business to give away your products for free, so I will pay for not only me and my partner's drink, I am going to pay for everything this group of kids' order." What once was mumbling words under their breath, and probably not very flattering, became cheers and warm smiling faces.

What happened next was even more impressive. Jeff asked the kids if any of them liked boxing or were interested in learning martial arts. Every hand in the group went up. Officer Sotherland formally introduced himself and said, "You can also call me Coach Jeff, and the guy standing over there with his mouth wide open for flies to fly in, is Officer Grimes, or you can call him Coach Rod. He is my assistant."

Jeff spent the next thirty minutes telling the seven- to thirteen-year-old youngsters about his career in boxing and why he got into martial arts. "If you guys want to learn, I am willing to teach you. Have your mom or dad come into the station and ask for me any day this week and I will share with them what my program will consist of." As the group scrambled away, I could hear them debating which training they would choose.

As we walked towards our car, a gentleman stopped us, saying, "I couldn't help overhearing you officers talking to that group of kids, and I was very moved by the interaction and dialogue." He introduced himself as Mr. Allen Pearson. He worked downtown at the Michcon energy company, which was our natural gas provider. One of his roles there was overseeing the charitable dollars the company disperses back into the community. "I would really like to have a sit-down meeting and see if Michcon can help you guys out with some funding." Jeff replied, "I would love to have that opportunity," and took the business card Mr. Pearson was passing him. The conversation was interrupted by the voice of the dispatcher, "5-cruiser. Attention cars in the 5th district. We are receiving multiple tickets from 911. 12415 Gratiot Ave, at the Ford dealership, a man is inside with a shotgun, possible holdup in progress." I jumped in, "very nice meeting you sir, but we have to go." It was not our call, but when there are multiple tickets on a call, you could best bet it was a good call.

Minutes later, I was further impressed with my new partner as he demonstrated his driving skills. The patrol vehicle came squealing to a stop at the dealership. The crew from 5-cruiser was already on location. Because they were a plain clothes crew, it was good training, and in fact, new department policy that the first uniform officers on their scene contact them as soon as possible, especially if it was a gun call.

As we made our way inside the building, we were greeted by several customers and employees running out past us. Jeff and I moved towards the direction they were coming from, which was the service area. We noticed blood on the floor in the hallway leading from a side office near the service area. Once inside the service area, I spotted two of the four members from the 5-cruiser crew providing CPR to a female victim. One of the officers yelled out, "Request EMS; she has a gunshot wound to the back. The suspect ran out of the rear door, my other two partners went out there looking for him." I headed towards the rear door while Officer Sotherland stayed with the two and the victim.

Once outside in the rear, I saw the two officers talking to a group of people. "Hey Grimes." one said to me, "this is what we have so far. The shooter is a white male," and he continued with a full description. It appeared that the shooter and the victim were married but separated. As I headed back inside, I began to put the full description of the suspect over the air, including the type of vehicle some of the witnesses saw him escape in. Several more patrol units arrived, and a few minutes later, EMS was on the scene, as well as a Sergeant.

Jeff walked over to me and said, "She is gone. She took a shotgun blast to the back from pretty close range. She made it from her office down the hall to here before collapsing. While you were outside, I spoke with the manager. He shared with me that they were having big marital problems because her husband had begun to drink quite heavily, plus she thought he was cheating on her, and that was the reason for them separating." Jeff went on to say that the manager shared the husband had come up there on a few other occasions and appeared to be drunk. Both times, his visits ended with them auguring very loudly and him threatening to kill her.

"I guess we can go back in service; there's nothing more we can do here. The homicide team is en route from downtown."

Damn! What a terrible way to go. Hopefully, we will get this guy pretty quick, I thought. The dispatcher's voice came over the air, "All units. All units. Additional information on the person wanted for the shooting at the Ford dealership. Be advised the suspect is a Detroit Firefighter." "Wow!" came out of my mouth before I realized I had said it. "I know," Jeff said, concurring with my disbelief. "After all, police and firemen are trained to protect and save lives, not take them."

More information continued to be broadcast by the dispatcher, including a statement the shooter called into the 911 center. "I know I have done an unspeakable thing and I know police officers and firefighters will be looking for me everywhere. Please don't come looking. I don't want to hurt a fellow officer. I know what I must do next, and I will. I will call back to the 911 center when I select my location where you can find me. To my fellow firefighter brothers and sisters I am sorry for bringing this dishonor to our profession. Please forgive me."

A few minutes later, a Police Chaplain came over the air with a short prayer for the soldier that had lost his way, as well as for all those that were out there looking for him, before he turned the shotgun on himself.

The manhunt was extensive. Assistance came from the State Police and the Sheriff's Department. Just over two hours into the search, the dispatcher came over the air, "All units. All units. The suspect wanted for the homicide at the dealership is in the parking lot at Logan Park located at the foot of Conner Street." "Shit Jeff! We are three blocks away. Hit it."

Seconds later, we pulled into the parking lot. Sure as shit, the van described by witnesses is right there. Jeff stopped the patrol car and we approached from the rear. I was on the driver's side and focused on not knowing if he had shot himself yet. Once I made my way to the window and looked in, I could see that he had already done his deed. It appeared that he put the shotgun on the right side of his head and pulled the trigger. I will never forget the visual of this scene. His entire head was blown off from the ear forward. It wasn't until I stepped back away from the vehicle that I realized I had walked through his brains, and parts of his skull.

Moments later, the parking lot was filled with police, fire and EMS vehicles. It was useless trying to keep everyone out of the crime scene; they all wanted to see if there was something that could be done to possibly save him. Others just wanted to see how he did it. Once the brass came on the scene, I said to Jeff, "Let's head into the station and do our report."

Chapter 21
Springle Mack And Goethe

"Shots fired! Officer down! Officer down," the screams kept coming over the air. "Dispatch officer down! Officer down!" "Oh my God! This can't be happening again," raced through my mind. After all, it had only been about four months since we had to bury two officers. The dispatcher, with a calm voice, said, "Settle down officer and tell me your location so I can get some help to you." The screaming officer said again, "Officer down. Officer down. We need help." I was sure hearts were pounding, ripping right out of every officer's chest, listening to his frantic cries for help. "Please give your location, just give your location and we will be there in seconds." The dispatcher again said calmly, "Officer, I need your location. Officers and EMS are standing by ready to come and assist you. Give us your location." "Springle between Mack and Goethe." "Thank God," came from Jeff's mouth. I slammed the accelerator to the floor, siren blaring with emergency lights flashing.

Officer Sotherland didn't bother to notify dispatch as car after car tried to get the air wave to let dispatch know they were en route to the downed officer's location. "Dispatch my partner has been shot,I am on foot chasing a black male who is still firing shots. The shooter just ran into a gray house with black trim." In less than two minutes, I turned the corner onto Springle off of Mack Ave., jamming on the brakes. Jeff and I were out of the car, running south towards Goethe Street, and the patrol car was sitting in the middle of the street. Three other patrol cars arrived at the same time. Officers were running with their guns drawn and yelling for curious bystanders to get back inside their homes. "Dispatch, four units are here with the injured officer. What is the eta of EMS?" Dispatch responded to my question, saying they should be turning the corner any second. Jeff and I continued running down the street and saw the second officer lying in a prong near a parked car. Dear God, please don't let him be shot too, I thought. "Are you okay?" Jeff yelled. "Yes, I am good," was the officer's response. Then, boom, boom, boom, came from the gray house. This guy was shooting again; there were at least 20 patrol cars on location by now.

Five minutes had passed since the last shots were fired. I could tell you a few years ago officers would have stormed that house hook line and sinker and this would have been over in minutes. The new department policy was to set a perimeter and call for SRT, (Special Response Team). About forty-five minutes had passed since this mess started and the injured officer had been transported to the hospital with word that his wound was not life-threatening.

Plenty of brass had arrived on location, including the Executive Deputy Chief. The SRT just arrived and now had incident control over the scene. That day was another dark day for our department.

The gray house had been surrounded for more than seven hours and no further shots had come from inside. There had been several attempts to communicate with the suspect by mega phone, and nothing. There had been much discussion about what the next moves would be. Some of the brass were in favor of sitting tight and waiting him out, while others were pushing for having the newly formed SRT squad make entry and bring this to an end. Either decision was going to come with some criticism. On the one hand, if we just sat and waited, this could have gone on for a few days, or how could we be sure when we went in what we would be met with? There were over 75 officers out there just waiting. That was a lot of resources sitting idle, never mind how much overtime was being racked up. On the other hand, if the SRT went in and there was a shootout, there surely would be those in the media and community saying the police department just wanted to show off its new unit and should have waited.

Finally, after thirteen hours of waiting, it was six o'clock in the morning. The sun had just begun to light the sky and the decision had been made to make entry. A few minutes went by and then you could hear the SRT commander barking out commands to his unit. Two six-officer teams began their approach to the house; one team entered, then the next. Regular patrol officers could not hear the radio traffic as SRT communicated on their own channel. Three minutes had passed since the teams entered the house; all was silent, then suddenly, there was a fury of gunfire. Seconds later, SRT officers were retreating from the house. An officer from one of the teams had taken a round. "Bring the EMS up now! Officer down." In no time they had him loaded into the rig and several police vehicles were escorting it towards the hospital. Unfortunately, it was to no avail. I could see that the officer was already dead. The round hit him square in the nose and his face was opened like a watermelon.

The Deputy Chief and SRT Commander were off to the side, somewhat away from other officers, but that did not matter. Several of us could hear their conversation. "What the fuck happened in there?" asked the Deputy Chief. "You assured me that you and your team could make entry and get this motherfucker. Instead, we have yet another officer headed to the hospital and he is probably dead as well."

While most officers had their attention on the SRT Commander getting his ass handed to him by the Deputy Chief, suddenly there was a loud yell. I turned to see what was happening and saw an officer running towards the house all alone. Several officers are screaming, "No, no, come back! Do not go in there!" It turned out that the officer running towards the house was a Lieutenant and the father of the fallen officer from the SRT squad.

As soon as the Lieutenant hit the porch, one shot rang out and the Lieutenant was blown back. He was dead before he hit the ground. Officers from everywhere opened fire on the house. The Deputy Chief was yelling, "Seize fire, seize fire, damn it! Get the armor car up here so we can have cover to retrieve that officer's body." As the armor car pulled into position, a team of officers recovered the lifeless body.

I could not believe what I just witnessed, or any of this as a matter of fact. My mind was somewhat frozen as I fought to stay present in the situation, which was there was a man inside that house willing to kill police officers. The scene was quite chaotic; officers were crying, some cursing, while many were in shock. I could never imagine a scene becoming this unorganized with top brass present and officers acting with reckless actions.

Things had finally settled down and order was restored among the troops. What a crazy thing to say when referring to police officers. I was sure more than 200 rounds were fired into the house by officers. I refrained from joining in for two reasons. Number one, I did not see a threatening target, and secondly, we still didn't know if there were innocent people trapped inside that house.

The Deputy Chief instructed all Sergeants on the scene to monitor officers assigned to their squads and all ranking officers, Lieutenants and above, "I want you inside the mobile command post NOW!" My God, will this ever end? I thought. Two officers were dead and one was wounded. I fought to keep the visual of the Lieutenant's body being blown off the porch. This guy must have had a high-power rifle.

This standoff had gone past the 20-hour mark, with no signs it would end anytime soon. Suddenly, a single shot from what sounded like a smaller caliber gun was heard from what appeared to be in an upstairs room at the rear of the house. Moments later, there were crying screams from a woman's voice, "Please do not shoot! Please don't shoot me," as she came running out the front door. "He shot himself in the head. Oh my God, oh my God!" "Get on the ground! Get on the ground NOW," several officers were yelling at this unknown woman. She stopped with her hands high in the air, screaming, "Please don't shoot me. Please don't shoot me." Officers moved in quickly and took her from in front of the house.

The SRT Commander and several of his officers entered the house again. A few minutes later, the Commander reappeared on the front porch and gave a thumbs-down hand signal to the Deputy Chief, indicating that the shooter was dead.

What a mess! Homicide and Internal Affairs had their work cut for them with this one. Every officer who fired his or her weapon would have to be interviewed. The evidence techs would have a more challenging job because they would have to try and locate and identify every bullet fired. That was just the beginning of things; many officers would surely need to see a psychiatrist to deal with the emotional trauma they suffered.

It was Thursday. Four days had passed since the shootout, and the funerals were scheduled that day and the day after that. I just needed to keep it together until then; my furlough started Saturday.

I had not made plans to go anywhere, instead I was just planning on getting some much-needed work done around the house. I spent the next two weeks doing just that.

Chapter 22
New Year's Eve Shotgun

Time flies when you are on vacation, and my two weeks were breezed by in a flash. We were back in the saddle. Officer Sotherland informed me that while I was off, he had signed up five more kids for the boxing and martial arts program. That was added to the seven we signed in the beginning, giving us an even dozen. We were working the midnight to 8:00 am shift. Our time in the gym with kids was from 6 pm to 8 pm, making for a sleep-broken schedule. I got to the patrol car first and jumped in on the passenger side. Moments later, Jeff walked up, "Really," he muttered. "You have been off for two weeks and you are making me drive your first day back." "Yes, yes, I am," was my reply in a laughing voice. The shift passed by rather quickly with not much going on, the usual alarm calls, nothing more. The entire month on midnight's was quiet, as was the next couple of months.

With Christmas behind us, we were ready to turn the calendar to another year. New Year's Eve on afternoons was always busy, with plenty of gun runs and drunks. This day was no different. We had only been on the streets for an hour when we heard a volley of gunfire sounding like it was only a block away. "Jesus, they have started already." For whatever reason, folks in this town liked to shoot their guns on New Year's Eve to ring in the New Year. "Yeah. It's crazy Rod. I don't get it either, but maybe we should take a look to make sure no one is lying in the street."

After checking the area and finding nothing, we decided to request a lunch break. It was only one and a half hours into the shift, but once things got going, we would be hopping for the remainder of the night. Jeff suggested we eat at McMurry's, which was a nice steakhouse. "I'd like to have a steak for dinner on the last day of the year," he said. "Okay that works for me." Not having a reservation, the wait staff went the extra mile and created a small space for us off to the side, for which we were very thankful.

As we were walking back to our patrol car with full stomachs, I remarked, "Thanks partner. That was a great choice. My meal was excellent, how about yours?" He laughed and said, "Did you notice I was not doing much talking while there was food on my plate?"

We got back in the car and Officer Sotherland notified dispatch we were in service and available. Before Jeff could put the mic down, dispatch was giving us a run. "Scout 5-8. Check the area of Jefferson and Lakewood. Caller reporting seeing a white male walking down the street with a shotgun." No further description was given. Jeff replied, "5-8 en route dispatch." Really? It was seven-thirty and someone was walking around with a big ass shotgun. What a city. We searched the area for several minutes and not able to locate anyone, so we cleared the call. The next few hours were fast and furious with call after call. It was around 10:30 pm; we made a traffic stop. Ironically, we were back on Lakewood Street, not far from Jefferson Ave. I was at the driver's car door talking to the driver and Jeff was standing off to the side providing cover when he yelled, "Gun walker across the street." I turned my attention in the direction Jeff was pointing and sure enough, there was a white male walking into the apartment building. I told the driver of the vehicle to get out of there as I drew my weapon while running across the street towards the building. Jeff was on my heels and notifying dispatch as we ran.

Once inside the apartment building, we encountered several people standing in the hallway. Seemingly, all the apartment doors were open, and it was one big party. I asked a few of them which way the white male went, and they pretty much ignored me. Clearly, I could see that he wasn't mixed in with the party goers as they were all black.

Moments later, several other units were at our location and we searched the four-story building from bottom to top with no luck finding our guy. At 11:15 pm, it was time to head into the station before the real shooting got started. Most would wait until the clock strikes midnight, but some would begin earlier. The Commander had strict orders about being back at the station by 11:30 pm on New Year's Eve. He would always say, "I do not want to give them easy targets if they are looking to shoot a cop."

It was a week into the New Year; the weather was nasty, snowing and cold four degrees, but at least the streets were quiet. Jeff started talking about one of the young guys in the boxing program, Manny Rios. "This kid has something special about him. I think we can groom him for AAU's coming this fall." "Wow, you think he is that good huh?" Sotherland went on to rave about how Manny had the potential to compete for a spot on the U.S. Olympic team. "Man, that would be something, and to think you found him at an ice cream stand." I chanted a little jingle, "I scream, you scream, a left hook followed by a right cross by Manny and they all will scream."

Our conversation was interrupted by the radio. Dispatch was asking for a unit to volunteer to transport the daily paperwork down to headquarters from our station. Jeff grabbed the mic, "Dispatch scout 5-8 will take that sir." "Thanks, scout 5-8," is the response from the dispatcher. "I will show you busy on a detail."

Before I could ask why he would want to be a paper runner, that was what we call crews that always volunteer to handle deliveries. Jeff said, “I need to stop in to see Mr. Pearson while we are downtown.”

After a short visit to headquarters, we drove over to the Michcon building, where Mr. Pearson’s office was located. I had never been past the first floor of this building. The elevator doors opened and so did my mouth. “Damn, so this is how the serious money do it.” Jeff laughed and then made a smart remark, “Act like you’ve seen a corporate executive suite before.” I had seen executive offices before, but this was on another level. We walked over to the receptionist; she looked as if she had just stepped off the cover of a Super Model magazine.

“How may I assist you gentlemen,” she said with a smile that lit up the room. “Is Mr. Pearson available? Officers Sotherland and Grimes would like a few minutes of his time.” I was surprised at her response, “Really? You are only going to detain him for a few minutes? I was hoping you were going to take him with you.” The beautiful smile was gone from her face. My facial expression must have clearly shown shock because suddenly, she burst out laughing. “I am just kidding. Mr. Pearson is a great guy. As a matter of fact, if you guys were here to arrest him, I would run home and get my axe and pitch fork, then head down to the station and be trying to break him out.”

One of the executive office doors opened and out came Mr. Pearson. “Is Ms. Gibson giving you officers a hard time?” Before Jeff had a chance to reply, I jumped in. “Yes, yes, she is and I have had it up to here,” holding my hand about three inches above my head. “I think she will have to go with us.” “What is the charge officer?” she said with a stern voice. “Being absolutely incredibly beautiful with an amazing smile and a great personality." "That is not a crime," she insisted. "I totally agree, but those are three great qualities my future wife must have." "Careful officer Grimes," Mr. Pearson said, laughing. "She is a firecracker." "Oh, okay. Makes that four things she has that my wife should possess." Ms. Gibson interrupted, "Do I have a say in this matter?" "Yes ma'am, you do." "Yes ma 'am," she replied laughing. "How old do you think I am?" "Come on in my office, Officer Sotherland," Mr. Pearson said, laughing while talking. "Let us leave these two alone to make their wedding plans." His laugh got louder.

Jeff and Mr. Pearson were only in his office for a few minutes before the door opened. Jeff said as he came out, "Thank you sir. Our program certainly appreciates your support." Looking at me he said, "Are you ready to go lover boy?" with a smirk on his face. "Sure, let's roll." Ms. Gibson or (Barbara) but in with that beautiful smile. "Thanks for stopping by honey. Dinner will be ready around 6:30 pm." The room exploded with laughter as the elevator doors opened. The ride back to our patrol area was all about the connection Barbara and I had made. "Yeah, and it was you that wanted to question taking the paperwork run." Now he was laughing hard. "By the way, Mr. Pearson gave me a check for $7,500. This was a great trip downtown."

We were back in our patrol area; things were quiet, but that was not unusual. It was downright cold out there. Damn, it was 10:15 in the morning and who did we see walking down Jefferson Ave, carrying a shotgun as if it was a loaf of bread, a white male fitting the description of the guy on New Year's Eve. I flipped the car around and came to a screeching stop about 10 feet from him. In a flash, Jeff and I were both out of the patrol car with guns drawn on him. "Drop the gun and get on the ground," Jeff yelled. The guy turned and looked at Jeff, then me. "Motherfucker, last time! Drop the gun and get on the ground." This time, he complied and I covered my partner as he moved in to cuff the guy. "He is secure partner." On my hand-held radio, I notified the dispatch that we had one in custody, possession of a firearm on a public street.

Once in the station and talking with the detectives, we learned that he was the prime suspect for several early morning street robberies. "Great job," we heard from a voice behind us. It was the Commander of the station. Getting this guy off the streets would make the Chief and the Mayor incredibly happy. They had been catching a lot of heat from the press, as well as several community leaders. "You guys will be receiving letters of accommodations for this hook."

Chapter 23
Knee Injury

"It will not be long partner before all this cold weather and snow will be gone." Jeff looked at me and smiled, "Are you trying to convince me or yourself?" "Mainly myself, but a little bit of you as well. You like this about as much as I do, which is not at all, plus the daylight is gone two hours into the shift." "April fool," Jeff replied, "didn't you hear the 30-day weather outlook is for temperatures to run 15 to 20 degrees below average?" "What a kill joy you are. My birthday is in three weeks and I am hoping for warm weather."

"So, Coach Grimes, when can I expect to see you putting more time in at the gym?" "I know, I know. I have been missing in action for the last few months. Barbara and I have been spending all our free time together." Jeff interrupted, "Yeah. That must be going very well." Just as I started to give him some details, a black dodge pickup came blowing through the intersection, nearly running into us. Officer Sotherland regained control of the patrol car after swerving aggressively into the curb to keep from getting hit.

I hit the lights and siren but to no avail; this guy was not stopping. I began broadcasting our pursuit on the radio. The streets were a little slick in places and the pickup truck was all over the place. He was having plenty of trouble keeping it straight. I continued to give our direction of the pursuit. Several other units were coming over the air, advising us of their location as we attempted to put a net around this guy. Moments later, the inevitable happened. He attempted a sharp right turn and cracked up, hitting a pole. In no time he was out of the truck and running. I bolted out of the patrol car as soon as Jeff came to a stop at the pickup.

We were mid block just south of Warren Ave. on French Rd. He cut left between the houses running westbound. I advised the dispatch, "I still have him in sight but I am not gaining ground on him." He was still running west as we crossed a couple of streets. I could hear the sirens in the area, but I had yet to see a squad car. I am determined not to let this asshole get away. It's personal for me. If he had hit our patrol car, we would have taken the impact right in my door. The thought of that gave me a little more adrenaline and I quickly closed the gap. The terrain in the open field we were crossing was completely snow covered. Just as I reached to grab him, I stepped into a hole and down I went. I bounced right up, took about five steps and down I went again. This time it was because my left knee had no feeling. A moment later, I saw a blue uniform flash pass me, and a voice calmly said, "I got him Grimes."

Minutes later, the officer came walking back to where I was laying in the snow, the suspect in handcuffs. "Thanks man," I said to the officer that I did not recognize. "No worries. Are you okay?" he asked. "I think I blew my knee out." "Okay, do not try to move. EMS is on the way." Several police cars were now arriving where I was lying. Officers were running towards me, asking, "Are you shot; are you shot?" "No, no. It's my knee," I quickly responded. "Let my partner know I am okay, just the knee." It only took moments for the information I put over the air to be mistaken for "officer down," which was the term we used when an officer had been shot. My transmission to the dispatcher had been that I went down during the chase.

The street was full of police cars. An EMS wagon finally made it down to my location. I told them that I thought I could walk to the wagon, but the EMS crew would have no part of that. "No officer, you are getting on this stretcher." The tech jokingly said, "Do you think we carried this thing way over here for nothing?"

At the hospital, I was getting most of the attention in the emergency room. There were three doctors and several nurses in my triage area. Jeff came in despite directions from one of the nurses that he could not follow. I could hear him saying, "That's my partner; wherever he goes I go." Jeff was acting like a mama bear and I was one of his cubs. "Doctor, how does it look? Is it broken? Are there any torn ligaments or cartilage damage?" "Jeff, Jeff, calm down," I said in a very firm voice. "Let the doctors do their work. I promise I will make sure you are the first to know the diagnosis." "Okay, okay, but I am not leaving your side." "Okay, only if you can sit there quietly." "One last thing Rod, should I give Barbara a call and let her know that a patrol car will be there to pick her up and bring her to the hospital?" "No, do not call her yet, I want to wait and see if they will be keeping me." The doctor chimed in. "Okay Officer, we are going to take you down for x-rays. I will personally let your partner know the results," he said with a silly grin on his face. "Okay, thanks Doctor. He is very protective of me and sometimes he can be a bit much." Chuckles from everyone in the room. Jeff remarked, "You all know I am standing right here, RIGHT?" The chuckles then turned to laughs.

"Good news, Officer Grimes. There are no breaks nor tears, but you do have a severe sprain in that knee. We are going to let you go home tonight but you will need rehab therapy. Oh, by the way you are going on restricted duty during your therapy."

Jeff was rolling me towards the exit door in the wheelchair. "Hospital policy at least until you get outside the doors. By the way, the goofball that we were chasing had just robbed the gas station up on Alter rd. and Warren. I found the gun in the pickup; it was an old rusty thirty-eight special."

Jeff rolled me towards the patrol car parked near the emergency entrance. Just as I stood up to get in the police vehicle, a red Ford Mustang came flying up to a screeching halt at the entrance. It was Barbara. She jumped out and was running towards the entrance doors. "Barbara," I yelled out. She turned in my direction and freezes. "Baby, baby, what are you doing here?" She made her way across the driveway towards us and I could see that stern look on her face. She was not happy. "What am I doing here? The real question was why in the hell didn't you call and tell me that you had been shot? Jeff, why didn't you call me? Why did I have to get a call from my mother after she heard about it on the news? "Baby, I am okay. I was not shot. That was a misinterpreted radio transmission. I fell and sprained my knee while chasing a suspect. I am okay." Barbara ran into my arms, screaming angrily but at the same time squeezing me passionately. "The news reported that an officer from the 5th District had been shot. When I called the station, they would only tell me that an officer had been injured but would not give me any details. I felt that it was you and feared the worse." "I am so sorry, honey, that you received bad information that frightened you. I didn't want to alarm you. Please don't be mad at Jeff. I told him not to call you. I wanted to wait and see if they were going to keep me overnight before I informed you of what had happened." "Jeff, I will ride home with Barbara and I will give you a call tomorrow."

Barbara drove away from the hospital with me in the passenger seat. I began to share with her the events that landed me in the hospital. Barbara was very quiet other than a few sniffles. "Baby are you okay?" I ask. "Yes, I am fine." she replied with a stern voice. "Come on, honey, please don't be upset with me over this. I wanted to know if I was going to be staying overnight before I called you. I didn't want to get you worked up over nothing." "Over nothing," she screamed. "Every time you go to work, I pray that you will return home safe and unharmed. I pray that I will see you standing in front of me and not laying in some hospital bed, or on a slab at the morgue. Any kind of injury to you is a big deal for me. How can you say you did not want me worked up over nothing? How dare you minimize my feelings and emotions! Is that what you think of me?" "Baby, you know that's not what I mean." Before I could go any further, she interrupted me. "Please do not say anything else. I just want to get you home." "WOW! Okay, I appreciate you driving me home." The rest of the ride was in complete silence.

Barbara pulled into my driveway but kept the engine running. "Okay, are you not coming in honey?" I asked. While staring straight ahead she simply replied, "Not tonight." This was a side of Barbara that was unfamiliar to me. "Okay. I guess I will talk to you tomorrow. Drive safe going home."

The last few weeks had been stressful; the therapy was very painful, and the fact that Barbara had pulled away from me had been even more painful. No matter how I tried to explain my actions about not calling her before I knew the diagnosis of my knee injury, she seemed to think I did not value her feelings. I hoped we could get back on track. This was her call for now, but at some point, and very soon, she would have to show that she was still interested, or I would have to reevaluate the nature of our relationship.

Chapter 24
A Change Of Scenery

My rehab and recovery took much longer than I had hoped, but I was finally going back to work in full duty status. The two months working restricted at headquarters was a nice change of pace, but getting back on the streets was what I needed. Barbara and I could not seem to put it back together, so I moved on.

Speaking of moving on, I reported to the Lieutenant's office after grabbing my gear from my locker. I just wanted to be brought up to speed on any updates before the roll call, but what I was told took me by surprise. The Lieutenant said, "Officer Grimes, what are you doing here with a puzzled look on his face? Your transfer came through about two weeks ago. You no longer work here." Shocked by this information, I stood there frozen for a few moments. Finally, I muttered, "Where should I be reporting to?" I had put in for three different assignments. "You should be over on Gratiot Ave. at Tactical Services Section," the boss replied. "Seems like you really want to do some serious humping. They are busting butt from the time they roll off the ramp until the streets are quiet for the night. You will definitely make plenty of money with all the overtime that section works. Good luck, Grimes," he said as he stood up and shook my hand. "It has been a pleasure having you here."

As I drove towards my new work location, so many memories raced through my head. Leaving Jeff as a partner was a big adjustment, but what better time to move on.

Tactical Service Section, better known as T.S.S., is a major response unit. Their primary function was heavy street enforcement, crowd control, and support for the districts that were overwhelmed at a particular time. This was a really good assignment for me. I needed to stay busy to keep me from thinking too much about Barbara.

I made my way into the base where T.S.S. was housed and the first person I saw was a former academy classmate. "J.T., what's going on?" I asked as I greeted him with a firm handshake. "Grimes, my man," he replied. "So, you are over here with us now huh? The bad guys had better look out now." Then he burst out laughing. "Come on, let me take you back to meet the Inspector." Before we could make it to the boss's office, we saw him coming down the stairs. "Inspector sir," J.T. said firmly. "This is Officer Grimes. He is reporting to us for the first time." The inspector lifted his head up from the papers he was reading. "Officer Grimes! Well, well, come on up to my office," as he turned around and headed back up the stairs.

"Come on in Rod and take a seat," as he made his way around to his chair. I was wondering if it was good or bad that he already knew my first name. I was a little nervous as I sat down, not sure what was to come next. "Welcome aboard. We are glad to have a good man like you join our team." "Thank you, sir," I quickly replied. "I am very happy to have the opportunity to be part of such an elite team." "Team is the key word Grimes," the Inspector remarked. "We do everything as a team. We train as a team; we workout as a team, and when we hit the streets, we roll as a team. I have read your file Grimes. You will do very well here." We spent the next thirty or so minutes just getting familiar with one another. Then he sent me down to meet my shift Lieutenant.

I walked into the Supervisor's office and found there were two Sergeants and the Lieutenant. Before I could speak, one of the Sergeants yelled, "Who the hell are you to just walk into this office without being invited to come in?" I was taken aback by the greeting I received and quickly stepped back outside the office door. "Sorry sir, my apologies. I am Officer Grimes reporting for duty sir." I was now standing there at attention. The room was quiet for about five seconds, which seemed like five minutes. Suddenly, the three of them were nearly on the floor laughing. "Come on in here Grimes," the Lieutenant managed to get out of his mouth. "Welcome aboard. Do not feel bad. We get all the new officers like that. However, let me be clear. This is a hard-working unit, and everyone depends on the other. That is why we are successful." "Yes sir, understood."

It was off to roll call and I followed the bosses into the room filled with about 80 officers. "Damn!" I was thinking. I did not realize the unit was so large. Without a word being said, every officer fell into formation in what appeared to be a preassigned position. I waited until everyone seemed to be where they should be, and then I took a spot at the end of the fourth rank. There were several officers I knew and more that looked familiar. The assignments were given and today I was the third man on a car, which means riding in the back seat.

I was rolling with two officers that I did not know, one black and one white. They gave me the 25 ins and outs about the unit as we made our way across town towards the area where we would begin our shift. The Lieutenant was not joking when he said we move as a team; more than forty patrol cars were in formation, aggressively moving through traffic. Lights and sirens were blaring when we approached a traffic light; the first two units blocked the intersection and allowed the rest of the units to drive through.

Damn, this in itself was different. In less than 10 minutes, we traveled across town to the 2nd district area. Then, like a well-rehearsed plan, the units fan out down different streets.

My partners were Hayes and Jarbrowski, or "Jaws" for short. They explained what our mission was for this area. Because there was a high amount of foot traffic moving dope, we pretty much were to shake down everything moving. I did not feel comfortable with the idea of what amounted to profiling by targeting young black men merely walking down the street. My comfort level grew after we were three for three on our investigations. Our unit also had a 44-passenger bus that traveled with the team. If a crew made an arrest, instead of taking the person all the way to the district for processing, we just met the bus and dropped off the prisoner, and then we went back on patrol. This concept allows the crew to spend more time in service.

Four hours into the shift, we moved to another area, and we stopped suspicious vehicles. This area had a high auto theft rate. We landed two stolen cars before the shift was over. All the units rendezvoused at Six Mile and Grand River, and just like we left the base, that was how we headed back. I was extremely impressed with my new unit and was already looking forward to tomorrow.

Days turned into weeks, and before I knew it, I had been at my new unit for three months.

Fall was in the air. My summer was a blur between traveling and playing softball for the department's travel team. On most weekends, I could not keep up with time. My roommate on the road, Preston, who also happened to be a Lieutenant, asked me if I would bowl with him on his Friday evening league. I explained that I was now working T.S.S., which he already knew, and getting Friday nights off was rare. "Don't worry about that. Who is your unit Lieutenant? I will give him a call and clear your Fridays as leave days."

I reported to duty the next day, and the Lieutenant told me he needed to see me after roll call. I was thinking that Preston made the call and my Lieutenant just wanted to let me know how to request my leave days on the schedule roster. I walked into his office after I had grabbed my gear. "Lieutenant, you want to see me sir?" "Take a seat Grimes," he barked in a firm voice. I was thinking that this doesn't sound like it's going to go well. "So let me get this straight Officer Grimes," he said with his head looking up at the ceiling. "All summer long you were assigned out by the Chief's office just about every weekend to play softball, correct?" "Yes sir," was my reply. He continued with his sarcastic questions. "If I am not mistaken, you are also on the department's basketball team, which means you will be assigned out some weekends during the winter. Correct?" Again, "yes sir," was my response. He pulled his eyes from the ceiling and stared coldly into my face and said, "So now I am supposed to let you have every Friday night off so you can go bowling. I have just one question for you. Are you a police officer or are you an athlete?" Attempting to lighten the mood in the room, my response was, "Well, sir, which came first, the egg or the chicken?" I was the only person laughing, and it was short-lived. The look the Lieutenant gave me was cold and without a smile, "Get the hell out of my office," he yelled at me.

I headed out to my patrol to meet up with my partners. I was thinking, "Boy, that was a bad idea to try to make light of the situation." Just as I threw my gear in the trunk, the Sergeant walked up, "Grimes, I need to see you back inside. Grab your gear." I followed the Sergeant back across the parking lot towards the building. He turned and asked, "What the hell did you say to the Lieutenant? He is pissed off with you and that's not good." I shared with the Sergeant my conversation with the boss. He dropped his head and said, "You know this assignment is a heavy workload unit. Everyone is expected to be here when it's their turn to work. You getting assigned out by the Chief is one thing, but having another Lieutenant call asking if you can be off on Friday nights really didn't sit well with the boss." "No kidding, he seemed to be pretty upset when I tried to bring a little lighthearted humor to the conversation." "Yeah, that was a bad idea. I have been instructed to reassign you, and trust me, it is not a good one."

The Lieutenant demonstrated that he had no sense of humor. My new assignment was walking a beat in the Brewster projects alone. This was a near-suicidal assignment. The Brewster's was a heavily infested drug area and most people there did not care for the police. Worse yet, my shift was from 7:00 pm to 3:00 am. To make matters worse, I was not given a patrol car. I was to be dropped off by my partners.

"What the hell did you do Grimes?" Hayes asked. "You do realize that the Lieutenant has written you off and doesn't care what happens to you, right? This shit is crazy. You need to call the union office about this," Jaws added. "Hey guys, don't worry. I will be okay. My folks always told me when given lemons in life, just make lemonade." Hayes laughed and said, "We will sneak by to check on you whenever we get a chance. Be careful Grimes."

I got out of the patrol car and casually began strolling down the sidewalk. It didn't take long before I came across three young guys. One of them said, "Are you lost Mr. Police Officer?" That bought a laugh from the other two. I laughed as well and reply, "Yeah, can you point me towards the nearest donut shop?" They laughed again but sarcastically and walked away. I heard one of them say, "He is an asshole." The sun had set and the temperature was beginning to drop. I could not stay out here for another five and a half hours.

I made my way through the apartment complex to the rec building. I could hear basketballs bouncing. I pulled the door open and stepped inside the musty gym. Suddenly, no balls were bouncing, and all eyes were on me. A voice yelled out, "What the fuck do you want five-o?" There were about 30 to 40 guys in the gym. I didn't respond to the question but just walked across the floor towards the bleachers. Another voice asked, "Where is your backup, because you are going to need it walking your ass up in here like you are in control. We run this shit in the Brewster's." I stopped and turned my attention toward the sounds of that voice, "Hey young man, trust me I don't need backup and as long as you aren't breaking the law, yes you can run this shit in the Brewster's. Just know that when you cross the line and I am here, I will be running this shit. You may have a gang up in here, but when I call for my gang, they will come and they will come deep. I hope we are clear." About three or four began to slowly walk from the crowd in my direction. Another voice came from the crowd, "Rod Grimes is that you?" The person asking the question stepped out into the open. "Damn that is you, Rod. What are you doing in here?" "My supervisor calls himself punishing me by sticking me here in the Brewster's on a foot beat assignment." "Damn, that's out cold. He doesn't give a shit about you," as he was laughing. Reggie announced to the group, "This is my guy, Rod. He is a hell of a basketball player and a friend. He is cool." I took a seat at the top of the bleachers where I could see the whole floor, but more importantly I could see everyone's movement.

The games continued and for the next several hours I enjoyed some really good basketball games. At midnight, the custodian came in and announced that the gym is closed, and surprisingly, with no backtalk, everyone gathered their belongings and left the gym. He looked over at me and asked, "What the hell are you doing in here?" With a smirk on my face, I told him that I was a scout for the Pistons organization. "I need to be in here until my ride comes to pick me up around 2:30 am." "No worries, I am usually done cleaning by 2:00 am, but you can stay. Just make sure the door is closed and locked behind you."

I repeated this each day I worked for the next three weeks. Finally, the Lieutenant realized I was not complaining about my new assignment and returned me to patrol with my crew.

Chapter 25
Off-Duty Officer In Trouble

"Jaws, congratulations on your retirement. You decided to leave without a warning, I wish you all the best." Officer Jawbrowski was headed to Kentucky where he had purchased several acres of land to build his retirement home. "Well Grimes, it's just you and me now." "Yeah Hayes, the streets are not safe now."

Looked like we were going to be on the west side again tonight; the stolen car reports were through the roof in the 6th and 8th districts. We made our way across town in formation as usual, then fanned out across the district. Within 10 minutes, we were investigating a stolen car parked in a vacant field. "This is a nice Lincoln," Hayes mentioned as we pulled in behind the creamed-colored Mark VII sitting on four blocks. Hayes got on the radio and requested a tow truck as I began doing the inventory of the vehicle and started the paperwork.

Perfect timing; just as I completed the report, the tow truck rolled around the corner. The car was hooked and rolling down the street in minutes.

"What do you think Grimes? Are you ready for a cup of coffee?" "Sure, why not." We found a nice diner on the north end of the district and pulled in. The waitress came over to our booth with two cups of coffee. I sent her back with one to be replaced with hot tea. She returned to the booth, placed the smoking hot tea in front of me, and, with a flirting smile, asked, "Is there anything else I can bring you?" "No, nothing else for me, thank you." I replied with just a simple glance upwards. She walked away, seemingly slightly disappointed that I did not take the bait for more conversation. "What is wrong with you Grimes? She was trying to give you some action." "Yeah Hayes, I picked up on that but I'm just not ready for meeting new ladies right now."

The break was quick and now we were back in the patrol car looking for suspicious vehicles. Over the district radio channel, "Units in the area of 6482 Evergreen, we are receiving information of an off-duty officer needing assistance." "Damn! That is at the most southern part of the district. I am sure by the time we get there everything will be under control." I activated the emergency lights and siren. "Let's go, I don't care how far we are away we will head that way until dispatch tells us we are not needed." Hayes accelerated. In a few blocks, he made a hard left turn and we were on Evergreen but still about five miles away. Our speed was approaching 70 miles per hour; we were about a mile away, and I could not see any flashing lights. I was thinking, "Where are all the units?" Moments later we were in sight of what appeared to be three men fighting, actually more like two beating the crap out of the third. Hayes brought the car to a screeching stop and I was out of the passenger door before the wheels stopped moving.

One suspect noticed our arrival and took off running between the houses. The other was so into the punches he was raining down on the off-duty officer that he was unaware of our presence. I was quickly on the heels of the runner while Hayes went to assist the officer. Through the back yard and over a fence, I was still chasing this guy westbound. Just as I got near arms reach, he jumped the fence into the yard on the left and ran back towards the front of the yard. Over the fence, I went. Then he was over the fence back into the yard we had just come from. Damn! As he headed back towards the rear of the yard, I turned without jumping back into that yard. Big mistake, because once he noticed we were in different yards, he cut across the yard and jumped into the yard on the right side. Now, we were two yards apart. This guy had run from the police before. In only a few more seconds he is gone in the wind. I headed back towards the patrol car and my partner.

The street was now covered with police cars and Hayes had placed his subject in the rear of our vehicle. Because this was a felonious assault on a police officer, we must transport them to the district.

I walked over to the EMS wagon to see how the officer was doing. He was beaten up pretty bad; both eyes were swollen just about closed and blood was still flowing from his mouth and nose. I let him know that I was unable to catch the second guy. He nodded his head and gave me the thumbs up. I let him know we would stop by the hospital and check on him after we had completed processing the prisoner.

Hayes and I walked into room 317, where Richard Mackey was resting. "Hey guys" he greeted us, "come on in. Thanks. I really appreciate what you did for me. Those guys were really kicking my ass out there." "No worries brother. We are glad we arrived when we did. The one asshole that is in custody gave up the name of the second shithead, so I am sure he will be in custody by morning. How are you feeling? What have the doctors told you?" "They told me that I should be fine but sore for a few days. Nothing is broken." "Well, that's good news. We will let you get some rest; just wanted to stop and check on you."

Hayes and I were walking back to our patrol and I made a point to mention that anytime there was an officer in trouble call, no matter how far away it was, you should start heading that way. "You never know what the other officers out here are thinking. Just imagine if we didn't go, Mackey may not have survived that beating."

Every year for the next 12 years Officer Mackey reached out on the anniversary of that night and said, "Thank you. You and your partner saved my life that night."

Chapter 26
Young Star

The year passed in the blink of an eye, and it was almost summer again. I was still working in the Tactical Service Section, but ready to move on to something else. The training was great and most of the officers were cool to work with, but I was ready to get off the streets.

Every Friday and Saturday night, our unit was deployed to Greek Town in the downtown area. Tonight I had the misfortune to work with the biggest jerk in the unit. The area was jumping that night; thousands of people were out enjoying the early warm weather. I suggested to my partner that we get out on foot patrol, which turned out to be a bad decision. As we walked with the crowd, my partner thought it was a good idea to shine his flashlight on the ass of the young ladies walking in front of us.

A voice from behind us says, “Really, is that what our police officers are out here doing now, being disrespectful to our female citizens?” The gentleman’s next words were, “I want your badge numbers, I will be reporting this behavior to my neighbor, Deputy Chief Williamson.” I obliged but my partner wanted to be difficult. Soon thereafter, our Sergeant walked up. The citizen told him what my partner was doing and thankfully also mentioned that I played no part in the foolishness. The Sergeant ordered Officer Radcliff back to the base and told me to continue the remainder of the shift on foot patrol.

I settled in on the corner near the beginning of the four-block strip. The evening was moving along very nicely; people were stopping and chatting and some wanted to take pictures with an officer. It was a great opportunity to connect with the community in a positive way. Time was moving right along when my attention was drawn towards the parking lot across the street. Right on the corner at the sidewalk was a couple engaging in some very adult behavior. I walked over and quickly recognized the gentleman to be a newly drafted member of our professional basketball team. "Hey, hey guys. You cannot be doing that out here. You really need to take that indoors somewhere." I was taken back slightly at the response from the guy which was, "Who says we have to take this somewhere else?"

I moved in a little closer so that my conversation was only heard by the two I was talking to. "Look man, I know who you are, but you can't be right here on a street corner damn near having sex with this girl. Yes, your job is to entertain the citizens of this community, but not everything you do is for public entertainment. I really need you to take this somewhere else other than right here in this parking lot 10 feet from the sidewalk." Feeling like I had given him more than enough reason to stop his behavior, I was surprised at his next comment. "And who is going to make me take it somewhere else?"

Before his mouth had finished uttering the words, I said, "Look asshole. If you don't take this bullshit somewhere else, I am the person that's going to make you go somewhere and it will be to jail you shithead." He took two steps toward me and the girl grabbed his arm and said, "Come on Jake, the officer is right. We should go somewhere else."

Now I was hoping that he wanted to take this to the next level. "You better listen to the young lady, Jake, before you get your ass whipped and end up in jail." He did not take the bait and slowly walked away. I knew it was time for me to take a break from street assignments. There I was, frustrated to the point that I was hoping a citizen would want to fight with me.

Chapter 27
Rap Concert Gone Bad

Days turned to weeks and then months; it was late summer and a major rap group was coming to town. The young people were excited, and the law enforcement community was concerned because this crew promotes violence and one of their songs says screw the police, but not in those words. Everywhere we patrolled, someone was yelling "fuck the police." It had become a movement and an anthem for the knuckleheads that hung out on the streets. On more than a few occasions, officers had found themselves baited into unnecessary confrontations because of that song. It had reached the point that the Chief issued a department-wide memo related to getting emotionally tricked and finding yourself answering complaints about your actions.

These were the type of events our unit trained for. We were a strike force team responsible for controlling the crowds at this kind of concert. We came on duty two hours early today and were deployed in the downtown area, mainly around the stadium where the concert took place. Several other units were assigned, including Vice Squad, Narcotics Enforcement, Mounted Section, Traffic Enforcement, and several officers pulled from each district. Damn, there were over five hundred officers deployed for this one concert. It makes you wonder why this event was approved.

Several Tactical units were called to meet with the Deputy Chief in charge of this detail including my crew. Ten officers, two Sergeants, and a Lieutenant rendezvous in front of city hall. The Deputy directed us to hustle home to change out of our uniforms and into jeans and tee-shirts. We were his special needs unit and we were given the code name Delta Team. I could tell you this type of assignment meant some things may need to be done a little unorthodox, if you know what I mean. We also knew that the Deputy Chief would take care of any complaints that may come our way.

Within the hour, we were all back in the downtown area waiting for further orders. Fights were breaking out all over the downtown area, but the Delta team was instructed not to respond to that stuff. Finally, the dispatcher came on the air calling all Delta Team members to meet at the stage door of the stadium. The Deputy Chief was waiting when we arrived. "We are going backstage to have a conversation with these gentlemen," he said with a smirk. "I want this to be a one-way conversation. Do you understand what I am saying fellows? They have their private security so just make sure while I am talking, you match up with one of them, and if they say a word, well do I need to say anything else?" It was clear and we were more than happy to obey his directive.

We walked through the back door and down the corridor behind the Deputy Chief like he was General Patton going to kick some ass. We pushed past the two stadium security officers and entered their dressing area which was filled with marijuana smoke. "DAMN!" the Deputy Chief announced to their surprise. "This is why I don't want you motherfuckers in my city, but I don't have final say about that. However, I do have some say in how you will conduct yourselves while you are here. Now, I am a reasonable man so I will let this weed thing pass if you gentlemen obey my request. It is simple; two songs you will not perform, 'Bitches and Hoes,' and 'Fuck the Police.' I will not have you getting this crowd fired up and acting a damn fool tonight. I am sure you gentlemen are smart and will honor my request." The room was dead silent. "Good! Have a great show!"

We left the room, giving each of them the look of 'I am going to beat your ass if this gets out of hand.'

Forty-five minutes later, the show started. The crowd was as anticipated, fired up and loud. Small fights were breaking out in the arena and uniform personnel were removing groups four, five, ten at a time. Our team was stationed off-stage to the right, so when the event was over, the band would have to pass by us to get to their dressing room.

The police radio traffic was nonstop. There were units calling for assistance inside the arena as well as outside, and fights were everywhere. I overheard the Deputy Chief on the phone with the Lieutenant in the communications section requesting additional officers be redeployed from the districts to the downtown area.

About an hour into the concert, the lead performer stopped the music and began talking. He was really working the crowd up, then he said, "Are you enjoying the show," to which the crowd replied with a thunderous cheer. "We know you love our songs and that's why we are here to give you what you want. However, we have been told that there are songs we will not be allowed to perform, and I am sure you all know what the songs are and who said we can't sing them." The crowd responded with an even louder cheer, followed by a chant, "Fuck the Police. Fuck the Police." The band leader said, "Yeah, that's just how I feel," and with that, they broke out into an even more vulgar rendition of the song.

The crowd was going wild. Officers were screaming on the radio that they were being jumped by large groups down on the main floor. Just as the Deputy Chief moved to instruct the stage personnel to pull the plug, a very loud blast echoed from the crowd. It sounded like a gunshot. The crowd began to run for the exits, and it was chaos. The band ran off stage to the left. Our attention was now on the crowd to see if, in fact, someone had gotten a gun inside and was shooting.

They emptied out into the streets in just minutes, and fighting was everywhere. It was more than two hours before we were able to get things quieted down and under control in the downtown area. The Deputy Chief was not a happy camper. He called for the Delta Team to meet him in front of the Omni Hotel, where the band was staying. His orders were simple. "When we get in their rooms make them pay."

The team fell in line behind the DC as he headed towards the elevator. The manager attempted to cut us off before we could get there but the Deputy Chief interrupted him as he started to speak. "This is police business; the city will be responsible for any damages caused by our actions." We made our way to the 14th floor and to the suite they were occupying. Three hard pounds on the door followed by a shout, "POLICE!" We could hear the sounds of people scrambling around inside. "Get that door open," the DC ordered, and I was happy to oblige. One firm kick and the door flew open. The team rushed the members of the band, and well, let just say that the DC's orders were carried out to their fullest. Then off to jail they went.

Chapter 28
Nelson Mandela Visits Detroit

"Officer Grimes, I need to see you after roll call," Sgt. Gray said as he walked past me going to his office. In this line of work when a supervisor or boss says that to you, the first thing that comes to mind is, "what did I do wrong now?" I took a quick mental inventory of the past few weeks and came up with nothing. The pressure was off my brain because whatever it was, it couldn't be bad. Twenty minutes later, I was standing at Sgt. Gray's office door. "You wanted to see me sir?" I asked with a relaxed tone.

With no buildup, he got right to the point. "Mr. Mandela will be in town in a few weeks and I am recommending you to be part of the detail that will work with the State Department on providing security for him while he is in town." Before I realized it, the words "no shit," spilled out of my mouth. I quickly followed it up with, "Sorry sir, but wow Mandela, and you want me to be on the security team." A week later, I received my credentials. I would be up close and personal with one of the world's most high-profile leaders.

Nine days later, I was standing in the hold room with arguably the most influential black man in the world. My mind was in awe of his presence and I was star-struck. "Snap out of it Rod. You have a job to do. Focus," I said to myself.

"Okay team, remember your roles are and responsibility," I heard the Commander from the State Department deliver in a strong voice. The delegation was filled with who was who in the Michigan political arena: the Governor, United States Senators, Representatives, the Mayor, and members from the State Senate and House. Mrs. Rosa Parks and so many other celebrities, as well as common people from the community.

We began to move them from the hold room to the main ballroom where the speech and reception would be held. More than five thousand people had gathered for this event, and every news outlet was represented, including print and television.

The speaking portion lasted about an hour and the mix and mingle went on for another hour. Finally, through the earpiece in my ear, I heard the order to take our positions. It was time to move the delegation. As we moved from the ballroom towards the elevator, the pace was swift, like a well-oiled machine. We had the delegation gathered and loaded them onto the elevators. Unfortunately, because of the swift pace, we moved from the ballroom to the elevators; one of the members of the delegation was left behind, the mother of the civil rights movement, Rosa Parks. As other members were getting on the elevators, I watched as Mr. Mandela disappeared from my view.

I felt someone attempting to walk past me. Immediately, my right arm went out to stop them. My arm was being pushed down, and a voice said, "Move out of my way." As I turned, my left fist was coming around to greet this person who was clearly attempting to enter into the secure area. It turned out to be the seven-foot-tall center from the Pistons basketball team, the same player I nearly arrested in Greek Town some months ago. He had seen that Mrs. Parks had been left behind, and to his credit, he escorted her to the elevator to reconnect her with the delegation. I could appreciate him assisting, getting her safely back with the group, but his nasty disposition and forcefully slamming my arm down nearly caused him to get what I so wanted to give him that night on the street in Greek Town. Once again, I gave him a pass.

Chapter 29
Rubber Gun Squad

"Good morning, Lieutenant. This is Officer Grimes. I had the pleasure of working in your unit a few months ago." Before I could go any further in explaining my identity to her, she replied, "Yes, Officer Grimes, how are you?" I was somewhat relieved that I did not have to review the entire two-month history I spent there to get the Lieutenant to remember who I was. "What can I do for you, Rod?" she asked. Even better, she called me by my first name. "Well Lieutenant, I am looking to leave the streets and take on a new assignment. I remembered you telling me when I was returning to my patrol duties you would love to have me come work for you as my regular assignment. So here I am checking to see if you have a vacant spot I could fill."

As luck would have it, the Lieutenant had only a week ago lost one of her officers to retirement and was indeed looking for a good fit for her unit. I put my transfer request in, and two weeks later, I was reassigned.

"Welcome back," I was greeted by the desk Sergeant when I walked through the main door. "The boss is waiting for you." I headed towards her office but was stopped by several of the civilian employees. "Officer Grimes, are you back?" one asked. "Good to see you." This conversation continued for more than a few minutes. Finally, I had to break it up and said, "If I do not get in the Lieutenant's office this may be the shortest transfer in the department's history."

A couple of knocks on the boss's door and a stern voice greeted me, "Get in here Officer Grimes. Take a seat officer." Before I could say another word, she lit into me about making her wait while I made what she called my grand entrance. "I told you the first time you were assigned here temporarily that I did not want you up in these hot tail women's faces. You need to come in here and do your job and let these women stay in their cubicles." "Yes, I understand Lieutenant. It will not happen again." She had to have the last say on it. "It had better not happen again."

It didn't take long to get back into the swing of things. The office was always buzzing about something. There were over 40 operators in the room fielding calls from citizens and police officers as well. At least once every 10 minutes or so, you would hear one of the operators loudly fussing at an officer or citizen about something. It would be, "Sir/madam I am trying to help you but you need to calm down and let me ask you the questions I need answers to so I can file your report." Many times, that request would only fire up the citizen even more. Many times, the calls could be very entertaining. There would be times when officers would call and not have all the information needed and the operators would let them have it. I guess that was their way of getting back at the officers since so many officers would call into the system instead of writing their own reports.

My first year back went by fast. One day, the Lieutenant called me into her office and asked if I would be interested in learning the process for reading (VIN) vehicle identification numbers. With no hesitation, I replied yes. "Okay great! See Sergeant Morris. He will be training you." Auto Theft and Recovery unit is a very busy part of police department work. My main role was to monitor the tow yards with weekly monthly visits to each yard, 16 total, and check to make sure all vehicles in their yard had been properly processed and removed from the system after being recovered. Many times, the officers had the stolen vehicle towed to the yard but failed to call the recovery into the office. So the car would sit there in the tow yard and the owner not be made aware the vehicle had been recovered and they should go retrieve it. This was where I would get an ear full from not only the owner because their vehicle was just sitting there but also the tow yard owners because they charge $20.00 a day for storage after the third day the car has been sitting on their lot unclaimed. So, if a car has been sitting unclaimed for, let's say, 25 days because the owner was never notified to pick it up, that storage bill is $500.00. Since it was a failure on the officer's part to make the recovery report, the tow yard could not hold the vehicle owner responsible for payment of the fees, so I had to call them and order the vehicle release at no charge. WOW!

Many times, the officer would get off with a notification, but if he or she had two failures to file a recovery report in a year, then I had to do an investigation and make a discipline recommendation to his or her commanding officer. There was an officer, Klien, working in the 4th district. He seemed to think it was not necessary to file the recovery report because there was no report filed for most of the vehicles he recovered. The tow company would have to cover all the costs. Finally, my recommendation to his command staff was a seven-day suspension.

Things were going very well on this assignment, then I was finally called to answer for the investigation when the guy spit on me a few years back.

I was sitting in front of the Chief with my union steward while the charges against me were being read. "Officer Grimes, you have been charged with violation of General Order number 72-17 sub section C: Mistreatment of a person or prisoner while in your custody. How do you plead?" Quickly I responded, "I am guilty sir, but with an explanation sir." This type of plea allows the officer to plead guilty and explain why he or she took the course of action during the event.

The Chief accepted my plea and opened the floor for me to explain my actions. "Sir, it is true I did violate a department General Order. During the arrest of Mr. Brooks and while in handcuffs, he decided to spit on me. My response to his actions was to punch him in the face, and in doing so Mr. Brooks suffered three cuts around his right eye which required medical attention. I know I was wrong but I was not going to let him get away with spitting on me and not feel some consequences for his actions. Mr. Brooks was sitting in the back seat of my patrol car when he spit on me, and that is where he recognized the consequences of his actions. Sir, I tried to knock his head off with that punch."

The Chief sat forward in his chair. "Officer, I will not condone any of my officers punching a person that is in custody and not resisting. Mr. Brooks was not resisting when you punched him. However, I have no expectation that an officer should stand idly by and be spit on. However, when an officer is in violation of a General Order, he or she must be held accountable for it. However, if a citizen makes the decision to spit on one of my officers, they should be prepared to suffer the consequences. However, my officers will answer for any misdeeds. Officer Grimes, my question to you is if this situation were to happen again during your career would you handle it differently?" I sat there for a few moments thinking about the question the chief had just asked me. Then a few more seconds elapsed. My union steward gently nudged me on the leg with his leg, encouraging me to respond. I knew what answer the Chief wanted to hear, and I also knew how I wanted to respond, and it was definitely not an answer that would have sat well with the chief. Do I tell the boss what he wants to hear, or do I tell him my true feelings? My mind was torn. Again, I feel my union steward bump my leg, this time more firmly. The Chief repeated his question even though he clearly knew I heard and understood him the first time. I have the ultimate respect for the Chief and my integrity has always been a pillar of my character. It was settled in my mind how to respond. "Yes sir, I would handle it differently." Before I could explain what I would have done differently, the Chief interrupted me and issued his decision on my disciplinary action. "Officer Grimes, you will receive a written reprimand to be placed in your personnel file for 6 months. If you do not receive any further discipline during this time, the written reprimand will be permanently removed from your file. This case is resolved." I walked into the hallway with my union steward. He stopped me and asked, "Why did it take you so long to respond?" "I had to make peace in my mind on how to answer that question. Do I tell the chief what he wants to hear, or do I tell him my true feelings." "I am curious. What exactly were you about to say?" "I was going to tell the truth. Yes sir, I would have handled it differently. I would have hit the motherfucker twice." My union steward just dropped his head and walked away.

A few weeks later, the paper trail made its way to my Lieutenant to be added to my file. I had put this event behind me; however, the actions taken by the Chief did not sit well with the Lieutenant. Her door opened and in a light lady-like voice, I heard, "Officer Grimes, can I see you in my office for a minute?" as she turned and walked away from the door. By the time I made it to her office door she was back at her desk and sitting down. "Yes, ma'am," I said as I walked in. With a tone I had never heard from her, she said, "Get your ass in here and close my fucking door."

WOW! I was taken by shock at her language. “Sit the fuck down officer,” she yelled. My mind took a quick inventory to see if I had done something inappropriate or wrong. I came up with nothing. I didn’t have a clue what made the boss so upset. She began speaking and I could feel the anger in her voice. “I just received the final disciplinary action from the Chief. He thinks your actions only warranted a written reprimand. This is bullshit. If I was making the decision, you would be looking at some days off mister. I am sure he went extremely easy on you because you are a member of the department’s basketball, softball, and super stars teams. There is no fucking way you should only get a slap on the wrist for what you did.” “Ma'am, permission to speak freely I ask.” “What do you have to say for yourself,” she asked.

I started with, “Lieutenant, I respect how you feel.” Then I sat forward in my chair and locked eyes with hers. “Now hear me and hear me clearly. I know that I was wrong in my actions. I immediately advised my Sergeant on the facts of that incident taking full responsibility for my actions. Even after the Sergeant tried to encourage me to alter my statement as to how Mr. Brooks sustained his injury. I owned my behavior and yes, it was in violation of department policy. I was prepared to accept whatever disciplinary action was taken against me, be it a written reprimand, one day, three days, five days, seven days or 30 days suspension without pay. I would have served my time, returned to my job and worked just as hard as before to be the best officer I could be for this department, but more so for the community. I continued; I need you to understand me. No one, I mean no one will ever spit on me and not feel severe consequences from me. Not you, not the chief, not the Mayor, not a family member and certainly not a member of this community can spit on me and not experience my violent retaliation.” She was sitting staring at me without speaking.

"With all due respect Lieutenant, I need you to acknow
verbally, so I am clear you heard and understand me." S
"Do you have anything else to say for yourself?" "No n
"Get your ass out of my office and close the fucking door behind you."

I walked back to my workstation thinking, "Well, I am sure my big mouth has just gotten me transferred out of this unit. So be it, I will never compromise my honest feelings on certain issues." About thirty minutes later, the Lieutenant's door opened. "Officer Grimes, I need to see you." "Damn!" I was thinking. "That did not take long. I am out of here." "Yes Ma'am Lieutenant," expecting to hear where I should report to tomorrow but I was surprised. "I need you to take some paperwork over to the Deputy Chief's office and while you are out, would you mind grabbing my lunch. I have already placed a carry out order." "Yes ma'am, no problem. Is there anything else you need while I am out?" I asked. "No that is it. Thank you, Rod." Wow, I guess she had moved on.

Months passed and the Lieutenant had been promoted to Inspector. One of the Inspector's duties is to oversee the entire department during after hours, 4:00 pm to midnight and the overnight shift, midnight to 8:00 am. Inspectors are assigned for the week and it rotates among the twenty-two Inspectors.

My Inspector was also attending night school to get her law degree, so she always traded her easier afternoon shift with someone and took their midnight shift. Most of the Inspectors would assign one of their officers to be their driver and my boss was no different. For her first three deployments, she used one of our Sergeants to be her driver. When her fourth time came around, that Sergeant was on vacation, so she asked me if I would be interested in filling in.

"Yes Inspector, it would be my pleasure," I was thinking getting out on the street again for a week would be nice. Although I would not be out there chasing down bad guys, it would be a nice change of pace. "Great! We start Sunday night." "Okay I will see you in a couple of days."

I arrived in the office at eleven-thirty pm and the Inspector was already there in her office doing some paperwork. "Hello Rod," she greeted me. "How was your weekend?" "It was good. How about yours?" "It was fine, but not this bullshit," she replied. Her tone and laughter had me rolling as well. "We will hit the streets in about an hour. I need to catch up on some of this," she said as she pointed to stacks of papers on her desk. "Okay boss, whenever you are ready just say the word."

A little more than two hours had passed when the inspector's door opened. "Rod, I am ready." We headed out the door into the elevator and down to the garage where her police vehicle was parked. I pulled out onto the street. "I just need to grab a few things from my personal vehicle which is parked right in front of the building." When I returned to the vehicle, the Inspector asked me with a surprising tone in her voice, "You parked your personal vehicle right there and you have the sticker in your window?" She was referring to a political sticker supporting a candidate running against the current Mayor. "Aren't you afraid someone will say something to you about supporting that candidate?" she asked. She continued saying, "You know how political things are here in headquarters." I quickly responded, "Look Inspector. With all due respect, I can and will support whomever I choose and give less than a damn who knows about it. If the powers that be don't like it and want to punish me by transferring me to a shit hole district and put me on midnight's, fine. I have been there and done that." "Wow, you must be totally committed to your guy?" "Yes, I think he is the best person at this time to run our city and he has 100 percent of my support." "Great, because I am supporting the same person," as she started to laugh. "I can't be that public and vocal as you are Rod. They would demote me if I didn't act as if I was supporting the current Mayor. Enough about that. What is all that stuff you got from your vehicle?" "I have my flashlight, clipboard and baton." "What do you need that stuff for?" she asked. I explained that the clipboard is for writing down any pertinent information and charting our movement throughout the night. "The flashlight, well we never know where we may find ourselves and having a flashlight is a must when working nights. Finally, the baton is an intermediate weapon if the situation arises." "That all makes sense Rod. Sergeant Highgate never brought anything with him."

I decided to take this opportunity to engage the Inspector about working the street, knowing that through no fault of her own, she had never worked patrol in her career. I asked her if she would be open to me showing her a little bit about what officers deal with daily, the disrespect and downright offensive bullshit they're confronted with. I further explained that my job was to keep her safe and not let anything happen to her during her tour of duty, but I would let her see firsthand the challenges a street officer faces day in and day out. She was extremely excited to be offered that opportunity.

Another responsibility of an Inspector is to sit on trial boards and render discipline action on officers if necessary. "Not having any street experience really put you at a disadvantage Inspector. Hopefully seeing things firsthand will help you in your decision-making process."

The week was flying by with not very much going on. We responded to a few domestic calls, made some traffic stops, and investigated a few suspicious individuals hanging out on a street corner, but nothing serious.

Saturday night was the last night of her tour and the police radio activity was too heavy to have her involved in them. I turned onto Gratiot Ave from the freeway and headed toward the 9th District. Traffic seemed a little heavy but after all, it was Saturday night. One, two, then three traffic signals changed and we only moved about fifteen feet. What the heck is going on up there? I turned on our emergency blue bubble dashboard light and pulled left of center and went around the stalled traffic. Well, I be dammed. Three stopped cars were blocking all three lanes of traffic and the occupants were out standing on the sidewalk posing for pictures next to a painted mural on the wall of a vacant building.

I was pissed off instantly. "Inspector when we get out of the car, I want you to stand off to the side and watch for anyone approaching me from behind."

"Hey, what are we doing?" I announced to the group of about 15 people. "Who are the drivers of these three vehicles left abandoned in the middle of the street?" I asked. Quickly the apologies started. "Sorry officer. Yeah, sorry officer. We were just taking some photos of this cool mural on the wall." "Okay that's fine but why would you leave the cars in the middle of the street blocking traffic? I need them moved right now. Look at the traffic jam you have caused." Again, the apologies came. "We are moving them now sir." Of course, there has to be one that wants to be defiant. "Who says we have to move the vehicles," in an aggressive tone. Calmly, I responded, "Sir, I need you to move the vehicles. They have been abandoned in the middle of the street and are blocking traffic." Clearly, he wanted to give me a hard time as he continued in his attempts to impress his friends. This time as he began to tell me that I couldn't make him move his vehicle, I grabbed him and slammed him face down on the hood of his vehicle. "Sir, I am patting you down for possible offensive weapons now that I am investigating you." The small crowd became very quiet, waiting to see what was coming next. "Mr. Street Corner lawyer, please tell the group of interested on lookers why I am well within my authority to do what I am doing." He tried to raise up from the car. I again slammed him aggressively back down, instructing him not to try and come out of the car until instructed to do so. "I need you Mr. Street Corner lawyer to explain that I have the right to check you for weapons for my safety." A few oohs came from the crowd. He once again attempted to raise up off the hood of the car, and again, I slammed him back down. "Sir, if you continue to raise up while I am patting you down, I will assume that you are resisting. Now tell the crowd what I would be legally within my authority to do to you if you are physically resisting my investigation, seeing that you are a lawyer and know the law. I simply asked you to move your vehicle from the middle of the street, and because you wanted to be an ass about it you may be on your way to jail."

His attitude changed. "I am sorry officer." "Oh, you are sorry now Mr. Street Corner lawyer. Tell me, do you have $500.00 to post for your bail? Do you have an additional $250.00 to get your vehicle out of the pound?" I asked. "No officer, I do not have that kind of money. Can I please just move my vehicle?" "Oh, now you want to act like an upstanding citizen, now that your behavior is about to cost you damn near a $1000.00. I asked you to do a simple thing. All of this was so unnecessary." "Yes sir officer, I was being a complete ass about things. Can I please just move my vehicle and not go to jail please?" "Here's what I need you to do Mr. Asshole. First, you need to apologize to my boss for delaying her getting where she was going. Then you need to apologize to me for being disrespectful to my badge, and finally, you need to apologize to this crowd of people for being a complete jerk." After all of his apologies were made, I sent him on his way.

The Inspector and I were back in the car and she was just staring at me, but I refused to look in her direction. I was thinking, "Here we go again, another lecture about mistreating citizens." Finally, I looked in her direction. She busted out laughing, "Mr. Street Corner lawyer." "You are funny Officer Grimes. That's a relief." She approved of how I handled things.

It is 6:45 am. The sun was rising; the radio is quiet and we were just about done with her tour for the week. "Rod, I want to stop in at one more district before we call it a night, okay? The 2nd district is just a couple of miles up the road." "That's perfect. We can stop there."

We were sitting at a red light, and a car pulled next to us, stopped, then proceeded through the red light. I was hoping she didn't pay any attention. The traffic light turned green, and I drove off. My speed was a little faster than normal because I wanted to catch up with this vehicle and take a look at the driver. I pulled alongside the blue Mustang as the traffic signal ahead turned red. We both stopped at the light, then again before the signal was green, this guy went through the intersection on the red light. "What the hell is his problem," the Inspector asked. I thought this guy must be an officer running late trying to get to work because clearly, he could see that we were the police. Once again, I pulled up next to him, and again, the traffic signal turned red. This time, we both were staring at him; he looked in our direction and drove through the red light. This sets the Inspector off. "That son of a bitch is just going to keep running red lights right in our face." Now I was hoping this was not an officer headed to the 2nd District. If he was, she was going to tear him a new ass when we get there. I activated the blue light and motioned for him to pull over; instead of crossing the next intersection and pulling to the curb, he turned left and onto the freeway. The Inspector was letting the curse words flow, "He knows we are trying to get him to pull over and he is just ignoring us." Finally, I said to the Inspector, "Do you really want to stop this guy, because if you do, we can make that happen." "We can?" she asked surprised. "Yes ma'am we can, you are the highest-ranking officer in the department on duty. You can do pretty much whatever you like." "Officer Grimes, get this motherfucker stopped." I got on the police radio and advised the dispatcher that we were following a vehicle for traffic violations and needed a marked vehicle to activate the stop for us. Several units were coming over the air, announcing they were en route to assist. The Inspector was amazed at the response. "Yes Inspector, when your radio code is broadcast over the air everyone is coming your way." Within twenty seconds, I could see red and blue flashing lights in my rear view mirror. The shithead we were following must have seen them too. He exited the freeway and immediately pulled to the curb. I pulled behind him, two patrol units pulled behind me and one pulled in front of the Mustang. I exited the vehicle and this guy was already out of his vehicle, aggressively walking back towards me. I stopped and assumed a defensive position. He was just about in my arm's reach and seemingly wanted to get right into my face. I threw up a straight arm to stop his forward progress at the same time yelling, "Stop asshole! Give me your driver's license, registration and proof of insurance." "Why are you following me," he asked. "You ran three red lights. Now give me your paperwork." By this time, several officers were surrounding him. He continued to be verbally combative but was complying with my directions. After passing his documents to me, I told him to have a seat back in his car. Of course, he refused, saying, "I don't have to sit if I don't want to." "Sir you are right, but you will step onto the curb out of the street." I gave his driver's license to one of the officers and asked him to run him in the system. I asked another officer to look inside the Mustang. I was hoping this asshole has some warrants but that was not the case. The officer announced that his record was clean. The officer came out of the Mustang with a blue Kojac light, the type of light police officers used in unmarked vehicles. "Are you law enforcement?" I asked. "No, I am the security guard at a large apartment complex. I use that light when I am patrolling in the parking lot." "Not anymore. You are not authorized to have this light; we are confiscating it. You can explain to the judge why you had it." "Judge? Why am I seeing a judge?" he asked. The timing was perfect. The officer returned with the tickets. I asked him to write this fool for running the red lights. "You can contest the tickets, or you can just pay the fines, your choice." He attempted to snatch the papers from my hand and ripped them. "You may want the other half sir," I said with a smirk. He just walked away. I thanked the officers for their assistance and the Inspector and I got back into our vehicle. "What a complete asshole he was," yelled the Inspector. "Yes, he was," I replied. "And you should know the only reason I didn't knock him the fuck out when he walked up on me the way he did is I remembered the conversation we had in your office about knocking that guy out for spitting on me." "Well, this guy was a real jerk, and he needed his ass kicked. The inspector surprised me when she said, "So Officer Grimes, if you think you need to kick some ass, you go right ahead and do it."

Chapter 30
Primary Election Day

Primary election day had arrived. There were 14 candidates running for Mayor and that day the field was to be cut down to two. There was plenty of nervous energy at the main campaign office. Campaign workers were on the phones making the last-minute calls, rallying voters to come out and vote for our guy. As I sat off to the side out of the way of what seemed to be sheer chaos, I noticed the big guy standing at the window and calmly watching traffic flow by. "What could be going through his head," I wondered. My curiosity got the best of me so I strolled over and asked, "Hey boss, how are you doing? You got to be going crazy on the inside right?" "Hey Rod," he said with a low tone in his voice as to be mocking my voice. "I am great! We have put in 20 months going door to door, beauty shops, barber shops, churches, shopping centers and everywhere else in between. Today is the day for the people to speak. If I am fortunate enough to have earned one of the two spots in the general election, we will hit the ground running in the morning, harder and faster, but for now I am satisfied with the message I pushed in this campaign."

At eight o'clock pm, the polls closed, and the projected numbers were coming in. Our guy was leading by a wide margin. Now I could see a little nervousness etched on his face. It was clear he would be in the general election, and it appeared that his opponent would be the only female in the race.

10:30 pm, the numbers had him as the clear top vote winner and now he was being identified as the front-runner for the general election. Fifteen minutes later, we were making our way down to the ballroom for him to give his speech. The security team was in a box and one formation, the lead officer out front and the candidate in the middle of the other four officers positioned in a box. I was in the right rear position, which was the control position. If shit hit the fan, my job was to grab and cover him using my body as a human shield.

We turned the corner and entered the ballroom. Holy shit, there had to be at least twenty-five hundred people in the room anticipating his arrival. Camera flashes were coming from every direction and my eyes were having difficulty adjusting. Suddenly, my training kicked in: keep my eyes directed slightly downward and utilize my peripheral vision to monitor the crowd. Wow! This shit really works. My eyes quickly adjusted and I felt in control again. The crowd was worked into a frenzy when the DJ changed the music to the song "Ain't No Stopping Us Now." Everyone in the room now knew that we had entered the room.

Everyone was attempting to touch him and shake his hand; many were grabbing and pulling at him. We were using several of the techniques we learned during our training with the United States Secret Service on how to break a handshake that lingers too long or someone grabbing his arm. Finally, we made it to the stage and the boss delivered a powerful message that fired up the crowd even more.

After more than two hours of hand-shaking and TV and radio interviews, we were ready to call it a night. Now that he was in the general election, on-duty officers were assigned to escort his vehicle whenever it moved. We pulled away from the loading docks, turned the corner and eight motorcycle officers fell in formation, four in the front and four in the rear. The ride to his residence from downtown took less than ten minutes. This drive usually took us a little more than twenty minutes. We pulled into the driveway while the motorcycles lined the street so no traffic could pass through. Damn, this was pretty impressive! Once we were out of the car, he walked out to the street and thanked the officers with a handshake, then retreated into the house.

Chapter 31
Making The Detail

The three months between the primary and general elections were gone in a blur. General election was near. The campaign office was packed with volunteers and the phones were ringing. I could hear conversations ranging from the color of the flowers and table clothes, to how long he should take off after winning, to planning for his staff selection, to when he should move into the Mayor's Mansion. McKnight came over to where I was sitting, observing the room and the orchestrated chaos. Each time the door would open, the entering person captured my immediate attention. "You are always on guard watching everything" McKnight said with a slight smile and a sense of pride in his voice. After all, he was to be named the police department's next Chief, and he was the person who had approved me to be a part of the security detail during the campaign over 20 months ago. "Yes sir," I replied, never really taking my attention from the unfamiliar face that had just entered the office. I stood up to reposition myself a little closer to the boss. "Give me a second sir. I will be back." McKnight could see that I was not comfortable with our latest visitor so he followed behind me. The heavyset middle age man walked over to a corner in the rear of the office and began scanning the room. I walked over to him and cordially introduced myself as a volunteer. "Are you here to help with going out to retrieve the yard signs that have found their way on public grounds near street intersections and on the grassy area of boulevards?" A little shocked that someone had come over to inquire about his attendance, he quickly said, "Yeah, yeah, that's why I am here." "Okay great," I replied.

"Let me show you where your team is staging." I escorted him into a back room which led to the rear door. I opened the door and gave him an encouraging shove. "If you try that shit again, I promise my hospitality will not be as friendly." He was a spy from the other candidate's camp. We had been warned during our many hours of training that from time-to-time spies would attempt to obtain information by slipping into the campaign office and recording whatever they could in hopes of getting something juicy.

"Great catch Rod," McKnight said with a look of pride. "I want you to know that the boss and I have been talking about selecting the security team that will go to the Mayor's Office with him if everything goes as planned tomorrow. I would like you to consider transferring over to the Mayor's Detail when he is elected. You should know you are the first person on the list that we have chosen." And just like that, I was on the new detail.

By the end of the day, the 22-person team was established. Clearly, politics and friendships had played a role. There were a few who had demonstrated throughout the campaign they were only there for personal gains.

6:00 am, Election Day, and all hands on deck. That morning, our rally point was the main ballroom inside the Renaissance Center. This was where our night would end hopefully with a victory speech from the boss. You would have thought we were taking a long weekend trip. Everyone showed up with garment bags, small pieces of luggage, shoe bags, and anything else needed for the several changes of clothes to take place throughout the day.

"Okay, gather around everyone," McKnight barked out like a drill Sergeant. "Listen up for your assignments." Wow, no rock was left UN-turned. Officers were being assigned everywhere, and there were more than 80 of us in that room. Three quarters of us didn't make the details initially, but those that were not selected wanted to keep their names in good standing for future opportunities to come aboard.

McKnight confirmed his confidence in me when he named the four-person team that would personally handle the boss. Two of us in the car with him and two in the trail car. "Grimes, I want you to be hip pocket for the entire day." "Holy shit, I am hip pocket," my mind was trying to absorb this in. This was the most important position with the most responsibility in the formation. Basically, I made the security decisions on when, where, and how.

Giving out the assignments took more than thirty minutes. We had coverage everywhere the boss was scheduled to visit and places he may possibly visit. Officers were assigned throughout the Renaissance Center, Cobo Hall, several voting locations, and even on the People Mover later that evening.

Chapter 32
Taking The Bullet

Two weeks had passed since the mayor was elected, and the city was excited about having a new leader. The buzz was loud, not only here in the city but in the suburbs and across the country. This Mayor was in the mega spotlight and everyone was watching to see how he would work to fix the seventh-largest city in America. Many staff positions were changed at all levels of his administration. Staffers were excited to be in his presence, getting in photos every chance possible and even when it was not appropriate, they would crowd in on him. Many times, I found myself out of position because a staff member wanted to be seen standing near the mayor. This was a growing problem for us on the detail, so I mentioned it to the Sergeant in charge of our detail. Then I mentioned it again and again over the next few months with no change in the staffer's behavior. It became clear to me that the message the Sergeant was sending out was not effective. Finally, I went in to see the Sergeant and voiced my concerns in my most colorful way that I could get away with in talking to my superior officer.

The Sergeant again acknowledged my concerns and promised to get the staff members on board by giving us clear access to the Mayor at all times.

Four months into his administration, the Mayor called for a full staff meeting. Over two hundred and fifty people showed up in the large meeting room inside Cobo Hall. The Mayor delivered his speech and gave his marching orders; then, he opened the floor for questions and comments. I patiently waited until there were no more comments or questions. "Mr. Mayor," as I moved over close to where he was standing, "may I have a word with the group sir?" A little surprised by my request he said, "Sure Officer Grimes, what would you like to add?" Then he turned and looked at the Sergeant. I took the mic and introduced myself for those that didn't know who I was. My message was a career-defining speech, and I wasn't sure at the time which way my career would go, but I was committed to making my feelings known.

I started with a few words of understanding, then quickly shifted to my point of notification. "My job is to make sure that the mayor goes home everyday and to make sure he goes home unharmed. I am dedicated to this task with my mind body and soul. The mayor must go home to his wife everyday even if I don't go home. I am prepared to sacrifice my life to ensure he makes it home. Now, I know that everyone is excited to be seen up close to the Mayor and I get that; however, you cannot put yourself in a position that creates a security breach for me. The security team must always have clear access to the Mayor. If someone was making an attempt to harm the Mayor, I need to get between the attacker and the Mayor. Too many times I have to ask staff to stand here or there so that my path remains clear. Well, now I am tired of asking with a gentle tone and I want you to be aware of the position you are placing yourself when you block my access. If someone were to present a gun or knife on the mayor, it is my job to prevent the Mayor from being harmed. I will happily step in front of that gun or knife. Now, if I can't get there because one of you are in my way, I will gladly sacrifice you by pushing you between the threat and the Mayor. You will become the bullet sponge because like I said, the Mayor goes home every day. Thank you for your time and attention." As I turned and walked back to my post, the Mayor just dropped his head. Now, the room was buzzing as my words hit a nerve. The Mayor's executive assistant came to the mic and adjourned the meeting.

We headed to the car with the Mayor. The short ride back to the office was in complete silence. Fifteen minutes after we were back in the office, McKnight, now Chief McKnight, walked through the door. I heard him say, "The boss wanted me here right away." The officer quickly buzzed the Chief through. A few minutes later, the Sergeant walked by and tapped me on the shoulder and said, "Come with me; the Mayor wants to see us." As we walked down the hall to the Mayor's conference room, I was thinking, "well your big mouth and honesty is about to get you kicked off the detail." Quickly I made peace with the idea of being assigned to some shit hole assignment.

"Come in Sergeant and Officer Grimes, close the door and take a seat," the Chief said. The Mayor sat quietly and the Chief said, "Quite a speech Officer Grimes. What makes you think you can say something like that to staff members? Why did you think that was necessary? Don't you think that was rude?" The Sergeant started to speak and was quickly shut down by the Chief. "I am talking to Officer Grimes." I quickly jumped in. "Yes sir, it was very necessary. I, along with every officer on this detail, took an oath to protect the Mayor at all costs, even if it means our own lives. I am committed, and yes, I would sacrifice a staff member if he is the only tool available to accomplish my mission. If I am overly committed then maybe I should be reassigned sir. Just one more thing, I made a personal pledge to myself I was not going to be the one to look the city's First Lady in her eyes and say we let something happen to her husband." I could feel my eyes had begun to fill with water and my voice, yet still strong, quivered at the thought.

The Mayor uncrossed his arms and leaned forward in his chair, "Chief, you were 100 percent right when you said Officer Grimes would be a strong piece to the security team. What he did today, what he said, demonstrates commitment for filling one's mission by any means available him. Sergeant, my question to you is why you were not the person standing up there delivering that message?" the Mayor asked. Now it was my turn to save the Sergeant. "Sir, the Sergeant and I have had conversations on how to deal with this issue. The Sergeant has mentioned things several times to individuals. He and I agreed it may have a deeper impact if it came from me because I have always approached my duties with a no-nonsense approach." "Well, I think your message was received loud and clear Officer Grimes," the Mayor said with the sound of approval and a slight smirk on his face.

Chapter 33
Angels Night

Ten months into the new administration and the city was still buzzing; you could feel the excitement in the air. Strangers were speaking to one another as they passed by on the street. Smiles were more common than frowns. Was that all it took for such a change, or was it more about the person and his vision?

Halloween had been a sore spot for Detroit in years past. The three-day Devil's Night period had gained international attention for all the wrong reasons.

It started out as kids being devilish by setting garbage cans on fire, potentially dangerous but mostly harmless. Usually, the fire would burn itself out, or the homeowner would notice it and pull their water hose out and take care of it. Rarely did the fire department have to be dispatched to handle things. As time passed and the city began losing its revenue, the ability to provide quality city services really changed things on Devil's Night.

Frustrated business owners and upper-income class residents got into the business of burning their property. Yes, you read right, arson to claim insurance money. Add this behavior to the skyrocketing "White Flight" white people leaving the city after the 1967 race riots, the city was in a downward spiral. Many of those who could leave did just that.

From 1974 through 1993, the city of Detroit was led by its first black Mayor. It didn't take long for the racial divide to be placed at the feet of blacks, never mind the inequalities blacks suffered during the leadership of white Mayors. When you add the oil embargo that took place in October of 1973 through March of 1974, major cities were crippled. Detroit, being the motor city capital of the world, was devastated even more.

Devil's Night went from college students from the former Detroit College of Medicine setting large bonfires to kids being mischievous to downright criminal activity. Burn your city property if you wanted out and collect the insurance money. By the early 1970's the city would experience more than two hundred structure fires, plus cars. This was no longer the deeds of misbehaving young kids.

The then Mayor Young began deploying city employees and volunteers to patrol the city streets for the three days. This action began to drive the arson activity down.

The new Mayor decided to lift the deployment of city employees and volunteers, feeling that the city was moving away from what was tagged as the failure of the previous administration to manage negative behavior.

The Mayor wanted to get out on the streets and see firsthand how the community would respond during his first Devil's Night. Six o'clock, we hit the road, driving around town. The Mayor got his question answered. Shortly before the sun went down, the sky began to fill with smoke. We monitored the fire department's dispatch, and one after another, for more than seven hours, fire trucks were responding to fires, 358 fires to be exact. The arsonists were back taking advantage of no one out patrolling.

The disgust was showing all over the Mayor's face and there were tears in his eyes. We turned the corner onto a short residential block; the second house was fully engulfed in flames. My partner pulled the car to the end of the block into the alley to ensure we would not get blocked in by responding fire trucks. As the Mayor and I exited the vehicle, we were approached by a man screaming, "there are people inside that house." Without warning, the Mayor took off running in the direction of the burning house. Oh shit, he is going to try and go in there. I ran behind him, catching him just as he reached the gate to the front yard. I grabbed him by the back of his jacket collar, stopping him in his tracks. "You can't go in there," I yelled forcefully at him. "Let me go. There are people inside." "Mr. Mayor, I am not going to let you go inside a burning house." "Let me go Roderick," he repeated. "Take your damn hands off me." Again, I stood my ground. "Sir, I am not letting you go in that house. My job is to keep you safe and out of harm's way. Do what you must when this is over, but I am not letting you go inside. I will go in but only if you promise that you will not follow me." He agreed. I turned and headed up the steps. Flames were pouring out of the upstairs windows and heavy smoke could be seen throughout the first floor. This is not what I wanted to be doing but I took an oath to serve and protect. Just as my foot hit the top step, a fire truck came racing around the corner. "Thank you, Jesus!" I said in my mind. Inside a burning house was the last place I wanted to be. The firefighters were jumping off the truck before it came to a stop; within fifteen minutes, the fire was out. Thank God, after they had completed a search, no one was found.

We made our way back to the car and continued to drive around the city. The ride was quiet and the sky was filled with smoke. My mind was spent trying to remain focused on my job at hand while I wanted to ponder the possibility that the Mayor may have me transferred because of the way I manhandled and spoke to him. Finally, I was able to put those negative thoughts to rest and made peace in my mind that what I did was the right thing to do, and if I was going to be removed from the detail, it would be for doing my job the right way.

Nine o'clock am, we are back at the office and the Mayor was holding a press conference. The reporters were relentlessly hammering him about not deploying city employees and volunteers. He responded as gracefully as he could and voiced that what happened last night would never happen again on his watch. Immediately following the press conference, he called all of his staff together for a meeting, which included the security team.

He angrily expressed his displeasure with the events of last night. It was made clear that he was disappointed with the advice he received from his Public Safety Director that there was no need to continue the efforts that the former Mayor had put in place. He continued to talk about last night's events, including the fire we stopped at. Once again, my stomach began to get butterflies. His voice is filling with anger. Oh hell, am I about to be thrown out and publicly humiliated? As it turned out, his anger was more about the bad information we received that there were people inside that house. He continued, "Not only was Officer Grimes ready to risk his life to go inside and search for victims, he forcefully refused to allow me inside. When it was clear that I was not going to be denied, Officer Grimes stuck to his mission and calmed me with reasoning. This is the action of an employee willing to do what is right even if the boss disagrees. Officer Grimes, I salute you for your service." Wow, that was not expected and a wide smile came across my face.

Chapter 34
The Promotion

The first year of the mayor's administration was coming to an end. Rumors were flying all over the place about promotions within the police department, everyone was excited since there had been no promotions in more than six years. I was sitting number 191 on the Sergeant's list, but there had been several officers retiring since the exam, so maybe I had moved up quite a bit. The latest word was there would be sixty-five Sergeants made, so I still would be more than a hundred away. The good news was that we had recently taken a new promotional exam, but all the processes had not been completed to create a new list. I knew that my score on the written portion was good and I was number 42.

We had three Sergeants in the unit in line to be promoted to the rank of Lieutenant, so we needed at least three replacements. The Mayor's detail was a super sensitive assignment for both obvious reasons and some not so obvious ones. The non-obvious ones included how well the officer would interact with the Mayor and his family and if the Mayor would feel the comfort level needed to trust the officer with his life. These intangible details were most important.

A week later, the list had been created but not released, and I was not on the list. Bummer. There would only be thirty-eight Sergeant slots filled, but wait, I saw a name on the list and he was not even eligible. I knew that he and the Chief were close friends but this was violating the collective bargaining agreement. I didn't want to come across as a spoiled whining brat but I wanted to know how he was selected over those that have met all the requirements.

I stopped in the Sergeant's office a few days later and asked the question. He told me that there is a provision in the city charter that allows the Chief to promote someone if they have special skills pertaining to their assignment and replacing them would not bring hardship to the unit. "Since there is a need to fill three Sergeant spots, the personnel should come from the officers that are here and Officer McDaniels has the highest seniority. So, he was chosen to fill the third Sergeant's position." "So why wasn't I given any consideration?" "Rod, you were not on the promotion list and you have less seniority than Jerry. That is why he was chosen over you."

"You probably should check the list again; I am on the old list. I am number 191, I know it low but I am on there. I am sure that will trump someone that is not on the list at all." "Yes, it does. I didn't look that far down when I was checking for people in our unit. Let me get this information to the Chief's office today."

The Commanding Officer came walking back through the door. "Grimes, I need to see you." I followed him into his private office. "The Chief is going to make it happen. You are going to be promoted from the current list. You are pretty low but the Mayor told the Chief to pull you onto the promotion list."

Two weeks later, I was assigned to the supervisor's training school. What a great Christmas gift! One month later, I was back working in the Mayor's office as a Sergeant, or I should say, being paid as a Sergeant. I was already carrying out the duties of a Sergeant.

There was quite a bit of chatter around the department about my promotion because they had to reach so deep into the list to pull me, but soon after the promotions, the new list was created from the new test and I was number 35 overall. Five months later, 63 more Sergeants were promoted, so I would have been in that group anyway.

Chapter 35
White House Visit

The Mayor had become a rock star in the political arena. He had been invited to dozens of cities around the state and across the nation to come speak and share his vision on how to revive the city of Detroit, The city that most had completely written off as a lost cause. Needless to say, when he traveled, at least one member of the security team traveled with him.

The personal protection portion of the detail had 16 officers divided into four teams. The teams worked 24 hours on and 72 hours off schedule. The travel rotation was based on what team was working on the day he departed; the team leader decided which member on that team would travel. I have always believed in making sure each person has the skills to provide the protection needed to keep the Mayor safe, which will allow any of my team members the opportunity to travel and have the experience very few officers in our department would ever enjoy.

I created a travel rotation on my team, and to make it as fair as possible, we drew numbers from a hat. I even made the drawing as fair as possible. We used the date in the month of your birthday to determine who selected first from the hat. Now that the rotation was set, whenever the mayor traveled on our work day, there was no argument as to who was traveling with him. Some trips were returned the same day, and some trips were as many as 7 days.

The travel assignments, on the surface, seemed to be fun and exciting, but believe me, there is a lot of work involved. You are responsible for providing the same level of protection that he gets when he's at home in Detroit. You must identify any useable resources to replace your team members. With all that said, the experience is priceless.

I have traveled to Houston, Texas, New Orleans, Louisiana, New York City and others, but my first trip to Washington D.C. and to the White House was the cream of the crop.

The Mayor had a strong professional relationship with the first lady before the Clinton's were in office and even before he became Mayor. The President and the Mayor's political ties became very strong. My first trip to Washington was the mayor's fourth of the year. This was his second trip, the main reason being to meet with the President. You can't begin to imagine all of the security protocols and processes one must meet to get clearance to move around in the White House. I can't get into details about my movement around the place but be assured it was way better than the visitor tour you can buy from a travel guide.

While the Mayor was meeting with the President, one of the Secret Service agents gave me a special tour of the most secure building in the world. It was mind-blowing, to say the least. During my tour, he and I talked about protection protocols and I was pleased to know that the training we received was right on par with what they do. Their training is just at a heavier dose.

The Mayor completed his visit with the President and then a few more meetings with top White House staff members. The second meeting included lunch, of which I was invited to join them. Yes, lunch at the White House. Wow! Definitely something to tell the grand kids one day.

Later that evening after arriving back at the hotel, the Mayor and I were having dinner in the restaurant. His cell phone rang; it was none other than the President on the other end inviting the

Mayor to come back to the White House. This invitation was for the Mayor to be an overnight guest. With a huge smile on his face as he disconnected the call, "I am staying at the White House tonight, sleeping in the Lincoln bedroom." "That's great, sir," I replied. "What room do they have for me?" "No, Sergeant Grimes, I think you will have to settle for the room here in the hotel." I tried to make the case that I was his security person and everywhere he went, I had to be there with him. The Mayor laughed and said, "Nice try Rod, but as you told me a few minutes ago, the White House is the most secure building in the world."

We quickly finished our dinner. The Mayor went up to his room, packed a small overnight bag, and a short time later we were meeting a couple of Secret Service agents in the lobby. They introduced themselves and assured me that the Mayor was in good hands; they would contact me in the morning when they were en route bringing him back to the hotel. It was a strange feeling not having control of security for the Mayor. My night's rest was not as peaceful as I would have liked.

6:00 am, I was up, showered and went downstairs to have breakfast. I wanted to be ready when the boss got back to the hotel. At 8:45am, the Mayor arrived at the hotel. He made a quick trip up to his room and a few minutes after nine am, we headed to Capitol Hill for a few meetings. The day went by in a flash, and now we were in a taxi making our way back to the Reagan National Airport to catch our flight back home.

Chapter 36
The French Are Coming

Summer of 1995, the Mayor hit his stride and the city was on the rebound. All four of the professional sports teams were back in the city. Businesses were lining up to pitch their case for vacant land to build on and the number of families leaving the city has slowed. All things were pointing upward.

I pulled into the parking lot at the city county building right behind Sgt, Couch, our Commanding Officer. "Hey Dragon," he greeted me as he was ending a call on his cell phone. "How was your weekend?" I gave him the standard "it was good, nothing exciting" answer. "How about yours?" I followed up with.

We made our way to the 11th floor and straight to the conference room to get our weekly supervisor's meeting going. We made it through most of the meeting before the C.O. was interrupted by the mayor's assistant. "The boss would like to see you ASAP." That always means we have something hot coming to our plate.

Our Commanding Officer returned about fifteen minutes later. "Well, we will have a special visitor in the city next week, Sgt Grimes. Your crew is up." "What do you have sir?" "It seems the Prime Minister of France will pay our city a visit and he will be traveling with a very small delegation from his staff. The visit to Detroit is only for one day, arriving in the morning and departing the same evening. Stick around after the meeting and I will fill you in."

7:15 am sharp, the 747 jets taxied into the executive terminal at Metro Airport. Members from the Governor's office and a few State Senators are on hand to greet the Prime Minister. After about twenty minutes of greetings and a short media interview, the Prime Minister made his way to the limo. I was formally introduced as his security lead person as he and four others climbed inside. I gave the signal to the traffic enforcement officers escorting us back to the city that we were ready to move. The 16 motorcycles set their formation and we rolled away from the terminal, down a half-mile driveway and onto Middlebelt Rd. Traffic was being held in both directions and we were rolling at 70 mph. Onto I-94 and in less than fifteen minutes, we were arriving at the Marriott Hotel in the Renaissance Center. The Mayor was there to greet him and my team flanked them as they walked inside. They had a short meeting to discuss the itinerary. The Mayor left the hotel and we escorted the Prime Minster up to his suite where breakfast was waiting.

9:30 am, the door to the suite opened. The Prime Minister stepped into the hallway, "Sergeant Grimes, shall we go?" as he broke into a laugh. As we were walking to the elevator, he asked, "What is your first name? I would prefer to address you by your name rather than your title." "Roderick, sir," I replied. "I like that name. It is a strong name." "Thank you, sir. My dad named me after King Roderick from Spain during the early eighth century. King Roderick was the last king of the Goths. The Germanic people played a major role in the fall of the Roman Empire. Please don't ask me anything else about it because that's as much research as I have done on my name." We both laughed as we stepped into the elevator.

"How far to the Mayor's office?" he asked as we walked across the hotel lobby. "Not far at all, just a block away and across the street." "Do you mind if we walk? It is such a beautiful morning." "No problem, sir just give me a couple of minutes to reposition the vehicle and advise my team that we will be on foot." With a sigh of delight and surprise, he said, "Wow, usually when I want to change something regarding my movement the security detail goes ape shit." "Well sir, my first priority is your safety. I feel strongly that it will not be compromised if we walk instead of riding." "I like the way you think and are willing to make adjustments on the fly, Roderick. I will surely let the Mayor know." "Thank you, sir, but that's not necessary. I am here to keep you safe as well make you comfortable."

We walked through the doors of the Mayor's office and before the Mayor could say a word, the Prime Minster was singing my praise. I was feeling a little embarrassed but managed to keep a straight face. "Yes, he is one of my top guys but I don't want to say that too loudly, he may think I am serious." They both laughed as the Mayor led him inside his office. My team posted up to wait for our next movement.

We left the Mayor's office and headed up to the City Council chambers. All nine members were there to greet the Prime Minister. He spent about thirty minutes with them before we headed down to the vehicle. We were taking him to a large manufacturing plant located on the northwest side of the city.

Our vehicle package was a lead car, the limo and a trail car, and it was just my team at this point. The tour was going very well as they had been at it for over an hour.

The staff person from the Mayor's office who traveling with the Prime Minister rushed over to me, "Sergeant Grimes, I just received a call from the Manoogian Mansion. The Prime Minister's lunch is scheduled to come out of the oven in twenty-five minutes and it is not the type of meal that can be left sitting.

We need to get him back in twenty minutes." Enough said. I gave a hand signal to my team that it was time to roll and advised the Prime Minister that we had to move towards the vehicles with no time to waste. Without any resistance, he and his staff members complied. We had them back in the limo and ready to roll. I radioed the team that we were lights and sirens all the way as we had less than twenty minutes to get to the mansion, which was across town.

Now would be a good time to have those traffic enforcement officers assisting us, but that was not the case, so our best skills were put to the test.

We rolled out of the parking lot with me leading the way. The trail car and I would use the leapfrog technique to block traffic for the limo. Not having marked police cars made this a little more dangerous because other drivers couldn't not recognize our vehicles as fast. We made it to the freeway, and now it was pretty smooth sailing. We were in the left lane and vehicles saw the flashing lights coming up from the rear. They moved to the right to let us pass.

The last six miles were on secondary streets. Now, we had to be careful as we pulled into intersections on red lights to make absolutely sure that all traffic had stopped before the limo blew through.

Just a few more lights to get through and we would be back at the mansion. I raced by the limo to block the next intersection. The light was red for us as I eased out to hold traffic. I could see that there was a vehicle coming and I needed to let him go through the intersection before I pulled out to hold any other vehicles. I glanced into my rear view mirror, and shock and horror ripped through my body. My officer driving the limo was not waiting for my signal to proceed and it was too late to even notify him on the radio. The car traveling with the green light entered into the intersection and it was only a half second before the limo burrowed through at about 55 mph. My career flashed before my eyes. Had the limo been a second sooner into the intersection, the accident would probably have been deadly.

A couple of minutes later, we were pulling into the secured area outside the garage at the mansion. I opened the limo door and the Prime Minister once again praised me and my team for demonstrating phenomenal driving skills to get him back on time. My legs were so weak I could hardly stand as I kept replaying the vision in my head of those two cars narrowly missing each other.

I walked the officer who was driving the limo back outside for a private conversation. My first thought was to rip his head off for not waiting for my signal to run the red light, but it was clear from the pale look on his face there was no need to point out his mistake. We walked quietly to the back of the grounds to the Detroit River and stood there silently, staring at the water. We both knew that God had shown us grace at that intersection.

The remainder of the day was quiet and uneventful. By 8:00 pm, we had the Prime Minister back at Metro Airport. We sat and waited until his plane had wheels up; we finally called it a night.

Chapter 37
Presidential Inauguration

It was 1996, the Mayor had been in office for a couple of years now and the future of the city was beginning to look brighter. City labor unions were showing a willingness to work with the administration and businesses were looking at ways to come back to the city instead of ways to leave. Citizens were showing more pride in their community, and the overall feeling around town was that Detroit was moving in the right direction.

The President had been re-elected, and needless to say, because of the relationship the Mayor had with the White House, Detroit would benefit. It was a no brainier that the Mayor would attend the Inauguration. This was one of the few times the C.O. selected who would be traveling with the Mayor. His departure date landed on my crew's work day and one of my officers was next up to travel. The Commanding Officer, over the detail agreed with the Chief that a supervisor should travel with the Mayor for this event. I received the phone call. "Dragon," the C.O. addressing me by my code name, "You are going back to D.C. for the Inauguration. Check in with Mary to get the itinerary, hotel and flight information."

The flight to Washington was no different than any of my previous three trips; however, this trip required me to do all of my advance work on my own. Usually, I would have the aid of the Secret Service or the Washington D. C. Metro Police Department. On this trip, they had all hands on deck to handle all of their security concerns that come with the Inauguration.

We arrived in town three days before the big day. The town was buzzing like nothing I had ever seen before. The streets, restaurants, and stores were filled with people from early morning to late night.

The Mayor had meetings scheduled throughout the day and parties in the evening running deep into the night.

The Mayor was like a rock star. Everyone wanted to talk with him or be seen with him. He was a major player in the Democratic Party and there were some rumblings of him getting a nomination for Supreme Court.

Each morning, we would start our day with a three-mile run. Damn! That was always the worst thirty minutes of my work day. I was never a fan of distance running and he was running seven-minute miles. We were back at the hotel for a shower and a quick breakfast before we were off to meetings. The Mayor made time for the Mrs. to go shopping or sightseeing in the late afternoons, and then there were parties at night to follow.

Day four of the trip, the big day. 5:30 am, we were up and out for our three-mile run. I was thinking, "How does this man do this? How is he not interested in sleeping in until at least 8:00am?" I have been an athlete my whole life and kept myself in pretty damn good shape for a forty-year-old, but this fifty-seven-year-old man was making me question my fitness.

Today there were just a couple of early meetings on his schedule, then afterward, it was time to head down to the parade route. The sun was shining but there was a bite in the air.

We worked our way down Pennsylvania Ave until we found a spot that was pleasing to him as well as the Mrs. This was the first time I was ok with being in such close quarters with strangers; the people were providing some blockage of the wind and much-needed insulation. We stood there for more than three hours before the President's car passed in the motorcade.

I have to tell you, I could not make this make sense in my mind. We were standing outside in the cold for three hours to see the President's vehicle pass by when he could make a phone call or go have breakfast, lunch, or dinner with the man.

Finally, we were headed back to the hotel. My toes were frozen and so were my hands. I couldn't wear gloves just in case I needed to get to my weapon in an emergency. We had four hours before we headed back out to the parties. The Mayor assured me that he was not leaving his room until it was time to go to the first party. That was sweet music to my ears. I made it into my room and fell onto the bed. I wanted to take a hot shower, but my body overruled and just wanted to sleep.

It was a good thing I set the alarm clock because I had about forty-five minutes before we headed out. The nap worked wonders and I was feeling refreshed and sharp. My room phone rang and it was the boss. "Let's go," he said in his usual tone. We walked downstairs to the lobby which was bustling with people. The Mayor saw one of the congressmen from Michigan. "Mr. Mayor are you headed to the Black Caucus Party?" "Yes, yes we are." "Great! I have a limo. Would you like to ride with my group?" With no hesitation he replied, "Sure. That would be great."

We arrived at the location and there were a few handshakes in the lobby before getting on the elevator. I took my position at the front of the elevator doors and the Mayor and the Mrs. knew to step into the back. I was not prepared for what happened next. The doors opened into the ballroom and flashes from cameras rained down on me. The crowd of photographers was like vultures trying to get as many photos as possible.

I am momentarily blinded and I could feel the Mayor pushing against me to step out. I dropped my left hand down behind me into his mid-section, stopping his momentum. He quickly understood that I was not ready to move out of the elevator. It took about five seconds for me to readjust my eyes to the environment. I moved my hand from his gut and we stepped out.

Everyone was trying to get to the Mayor to shake his hand or get a picture. It was a mob scene. The Mrs. saw what I was dealing with, and with eye contact, she let me know that she was going to ease off to the side away from this madness.

After about fifteen minutes, the crowd calmed down and I was able to rejoin the Mayor with his wife. She jokingly said, "Is this how it's going to be when you decide to run for Governor or even the White House?" The Mayor laughed and said, "Yeah, right. You got jokes."

We made our way to four parties that night and the scene repeated itself every time. By the time we made it back to the hotel, I was drained. We spent two more days in Washington before finally heading home.

Chapter 38
Commanding Officer

Another year had passed and talks of promotions were at a fever pitch. For me, I was a bystander because I had just made Sergeant last year and was not even on the list for Lieutenant. Our Commanding Officer, however, was on the list and was surely going to be promoted.

I had been moved from a Crew Sergeant to an Advance and Training Sergeant. There were a lot of responsibilities that came with this assignment. The advance team was responsible for setting up all events outside of the office, such as setting the routes, identifying potential save houses, as we called them, knowing the closest level one trauma hospital to the site the Mayor was visiting, making contact with the lead person that is coordinating the visit, just for starters.

As the training officer, I was responsible for ensuring every member on the detail was properly tested, passed all specs of training and kept abreast of new techniques and equipment. There was always something for me to do. The cool part about this position was I frequently traveled to D.C. to train with the Secret Service detail that was responsible for the President and Vice President.

It is about 11:45 am. I was at my desk doing research on lightweight body armor and at the same time trying to decide what I was going to have for lunch. My cell phone rang. It was the Commanding Officer. "Q," another nick name I had earned. "Come downstairs. I am in the parking lot sitting in my car. I need to talk to you in private." Something big must be coming that he didn't want to talk about it in the office. "Sir, I am on my way," as I was walking towards the door.

I jumped in the front passenger seat, asking what was up even before the door was closed. He led with, "You are tuning heads over in the Chief's office." "Really?" was my reply, with a slight grin on my face. "So, you know that I am up for promotion this go round, right?" "Yes, everyone knows you will get your Lieutenant bars this time around." He continued, "So when that happens, I will have to leave the detail. As you know, the Mayor doesn't want anyone here above the rank of Sergeant." "Hmm, so the boss is going to stick with that deployment strategy and replace you?" I asked.

I had a meeting with the Mayor, the Mrs., the Chief and the Commander in the Chief's office. We decided that you should be the next Commanding Officer of the detail. "What!!! Are you kidding me? This is crazy! I have only been a Sergeant for a year. We have two seasoned Sergeants that are very capable of replacing you. Why me?" "We talked about all the possible options and this one makes the most sense. Both Sergeants Miles and McMichael are up for promotion in the next year, so if either of them is put in charge we will be going through this process all over again."

"Q, you are the most logical choice." I was blown away by the decision. He began to go over some of the behind-the-scenes responsibilities of the Commanding Officer, but my mind was still in shock. I heard words, but I was not processing any of them. "Q, Q, snap out of it," as he snapped his fingers in front of my face. "You will do just fine, but this must stay right here in this car. No one can know about this."

Interesting, no one was supposed to know about this but everywhere I went around the department, people were congratulating me. I found myself trying to pass this off as a myth, telling people that as soon as Couch was promoted to Lieutenant, the Mayor would change his position about no one above the rank of Sergeant being on the detail. But no one was really buying it. My mind was spinning as to how this information got leaked so fast. There were five people in the room when the decision was made and now, I know, and I surely hadn't mentioned a word about it.

Now that I was the Advance Sergeant, I rarely saw Mrs. This particular evening, the first lady was hosting a dinner event at the mansion. I went to assist the team on duty and be an extra body. As I walked through the front door, the first lady was standing there greeting guests as they arrived. She caught my eye and motioned me over. "How are you, Rod?" she spoke with a smile on her face. "I am very well madam and you?" I replied. "Don't worry. You are going to do just fine," she said, giving me confirmation that what Couch had told me was true. The nerves raced through my body at the thought of knowing I would soon have the full responsibility of the city's first family's safety in my hands.

Weeks had turned into months and no promotions had taken place. The rumor mill about me becoming the new Commanding Officer was everywhere. There was no need for me trying to deny it, so I changed my approach. When asked about it, I then said, "Yeah, I keep hearing the same rumor." Then I followed that up with, "I am ready to serve at the Mayor's pleasure, no matter what role he asks of me."

There became a point during all of this speculating that I pulled one of my officers on my advance team into a private meeting. I mentioned the rumor and he obviously was well aware of the talk. I told him that if this really became reality, I was going to need someone that I could trust as my number two man, and I wanted it to be him. I shared with him my thoughts on how he handled himself on the detail and that I like how he pays attention to every detail when planning out an event. I continued by sharing my vision of how the details would change if I became the new Commanding Officer. Mainly, we would become even more focused on the safety of the first family than trying to cater to the members of staff. No more running errands for staffers when our mission is the safety of the Mayor. The conversation seemingly went well and he accepted my offer if things turned out to be true.

Four months had passed and there were still no promotions. Something was up, but I was not distracted by it. After all, I was not seeking the role of Commanding Officer and the idea had moved somewhere in the back of my mind.

I was out at an event awaiting the arrival of the Mayor's car when they arrived and the Mayor exited the vehicle. There was a coldness in the way he looked at me and, noticeably, the very limited conversation he had with me. "Hmm" thoughts ran through my mind. "What is driving his behavior?" I did a quick assessment of my performance over the last few weeks and came up with no reason for his change in mood towards me. I had to admit this was troubling to me because if I was responsible for his safety, I needed to know that he could trust me and my judgment. While the Mayor was busy doing his thing at this function, I was able to have a quick conversation with the other Sergeant there. I told him my observations and the difference in the Mayor's behavior towards me. Sergeant McMichael tried to assure me that if I couldn't come up with a reason in my head that I shouldn't worry. He said, "Leaders sometimes show a different side of themselves to see how you will handle it." "Nothing to worry about Rod. Just keep on doing what you do." I took his advice, although at times it was difficult because I could sense some resentment coming from the Mayor.

Two more months passed, and finally, the promotions happened. Sgt Couch was made Lieutenant and transferred to a new assignment. What shocked everyone except me was that I wasn't named the new Commanding Officer. More shocking was the officer I had asked to be my right-hand man if I was chosen was chartered, promoted and named the new Commanding Officer. Wow, that had the department buzzing. Something in my spirit told me that I was not going to be chosen and I was perfectly ok with it.

Now I had to listen to members on the detail whisper behind my back about how angry I was and how no one wanted to work on my crew because I was going to turn into a hard ass and take everything out on my officers.

Sgt. McMichael was named Acting Commanding Officer while Raymond was away at Officers Training School, a two-week course. Once Raymond returned and assumed the position, I found myself the recipient of more unearned standoffish behavior. After two weeks of feeling like the new Commanding Officer over the detail was dodging me at every chance he could, I requested a sit-down meeting with him. I shared with him how I knew he was dodging me and that was so unnecessary. "Raymond," I said. "I am not angry nor disappointed that I didn't get the position. I didn't seek it. I was told this was a decision made by the people in charge. They changed their minds. I am ok with that and they don't owe me any explanations. My focus continues to be on how best to keep the first family safe. If you feel that I will be a distraction or no longer a good fit for the detail I will respect your decision if you transfer me. I have no ill feelings towards you nor any of the decision makers." With a sigh of relief, Ralph replied, "Thanks Rod. I appreciate what you said. I didn't know how you were feeling and I really need you to be a part of this detail."

Within a few weeks, things had calmed down and interestingly enough, the Mayor was back to his old ways when it came to me.

Chapter 39
Grand Prix

It was June and the Grand Prix had made its way into Detroit. The race that once roared through the streets of downtown had moved to Belle Isle, an island that is part of the city of Detroit and sits on the Detroit River between Canada and the United States.

This three-day event generates millions of dollars for the city's coffer along with hundreds of thousands of visitors to the city. This was a Mayor's delight. The logistics of security planning for all the events the Mayor would attend was monumental.

Our four person teams, which normally worked twenty-four hours on and seventy-two hours off, were working twenty-four hours on and twenty-four hours off. In addition to the Mayor's regular activities, Grand Prix events were scattered throughout the day and evening. My team was working as the support team on Friday and Sunday, which meant we would cover all of the Grand Prix events.

Friday morning started off with the Mayor joining all of the drivers, sponsors and other key officials of the race for a weekend race kickoff breakfast at Cobo Hall. There were more than fifteen hundred people participating, which was about a thousand more than I would have imagined.

It was a good thing we put a security plan in place for the security. There were politicians, celebrities, and VIP's arriving with security and there were people with guns everywhere. We took a page from the Secret Service playbook; we issued special lapel pins to any person registered with our department who will be providing security whether they are carrying a firearm or not. The last thing we wanted was to have someone taken out by friendly fire if shit was to hit the fan. The morning events went without a hitch, and my team turned the Mayor over to the regular crew for the day.

The big gala was taking place that night and the tuxedos and long black gowns were flowing. The Mayor was making his way through the massive crowd and he was getting the rock star treatment. Everybody wanted pictures and to shake his hand.

I began to hear chatter on the police radio that protesters were gathering a few blocks away. The protest had nothing to do with the Grand Prix but they were using this event in an attempt to embarrass the Mayor. This group was upset about the casinos that recently opened in the city - another good thing for the city to generate revenue.

For years, Detroit residents were against having casinos. Once Windsor Ontario Canada opened casinos, Detroiters could see how many cars were going there day and night. It was clear that millions of dollars could stay in Detroit. It was only then that the majority of the voters thought casinos were a good idea. Even though the voters passed the ballot proposal by 65 percent of the vote, those who were on the other side continued to be vocal.

"Priority, priority!" a voice came screaming over the radio. "We need backup. This crowd is pushing through our blockade." We discretely moved the Mayor and Mrs. to an area of the ballroom near our emergency exit point. I notified the officer driving the vehicle to reposition at the secondary exit point. I didn't want to take any chances. If this crowd became uncontrollable, I wanted to extract the Mayor without bringing attention. Not knowing what this crowd may do, I would error on the safe side. The party continued without being disturbed by the crowd outside.

It was Sunday and the big race day; the Mayor was ready to head over to the track. The drive was only about two miles from the Mayor's residence. He walked outside to the car and was greeted by eight motorcycle officers. The Mayor shook each officer's hand and thanked them in advance for being there. Once we were in the car the Mayor asked why we needed these officers. "Sir, Jefferson Ave. is a zoo and getting you across the bridge without their assistance would be difficult at best." The Mayor was not a big fan of utilizing extra police resources for his needs. Once we turned onto Jefferson Ave., it was clear why I had requested the motorcycle units to assist. They hit their lights and sirens, clearing a path down the middle of the street. A few minutes later, we were moving across the bridge. Less than ten minutes after we left the house, we arrived at our destination. The Mayor popped out of the car with a huge smile on his face. "Good call, Rod," as he gave me a wink of approval.

We made our way to his seating area, where several of his closely invited friends were already sitting. About an hour into the race, the Mayor wanted to go right down by pit roll. This area had very strict access where mainly the extra drivers and owners hang out. We were just on the other side of the three-foot temporary concrete wall. Not five minutes after we arrived in this area, there was a crash at the top of the straight away and everyone was scrambling to see which cars were involved.

I felt a hand on my shoulder and then the pressure of someone pushing themselves up to stand on top of the three-foot wall. I looked up and it was none other than Paul Newman, yes, the actor and race car owner Paul Newman!

His attention was focused on what had happened on the track and not on me. His fears had come true; one of the three cars involved in the accident was his. The safety teams rushed down straight away as two of the vehicles were flipped over on their tops with wheels spinning in the air. The crowd was as silent as church mice. Moments later, there was movement coming from both vehicles - first, the gold car. The driver climbed out and waved to the crowd. Next, the driver of the red car was not moving. This was Mr. Newman's driver. The safety team had now arrived and began assisting the driver from the car, and a few moments later, the EMS pulled up. They then had Paul's driver out of the car and place him on the stretcher.

Mr. Newman began to come back down off the wall and looked for my shoulder for assistance. This time, I was offering my hand as well. "Thanks, young fellow. That's a big step down," as he was laughing. "No problem, sir, glad to help." "Maybe I need to send my driver back to driving school. This is twice this year he has destroyed my car." He chuckled, shaking his head, and slowly walked away. Suddenly, he turned around, walked back to me and said, "Sorry, thank you very much for helping me up and then down off that wall big fella. What is your name?" he asked. "Sergeant Rod Grimes, I managed to get out." He looked me in my eyes with a serious look and asked. "How did your mother allow your dad to name you Sergeant?" as he busted out laughing. He cracked himself up with that one. "Just kidding Rod. You are a good man," as he walked away, again laughing louder than before. Now the Mayor was laughing at him laughing at me. The rest of the afternoon was uneventful.

Tuesday morning, my crew was back at it on our regular assigned twenty-four-hour shift. The Mayor's schedule was fairly light this morning, just meetings in the office. After getting the boss squared away in his office, I headed into our security office. I was greeted by one of the office officers, "Hey Dragon, you have a box here for you. It was delivered yesterday. It's on the table in the meeting room." As I headed towards the meeting room door, the officer said, "Somebody made a new best friend over the weekend." I picked up the opened envelope sitting on top of the sealed box. I turned around and looked at the officer as if to ask why it was opened, but he quickly said, "It was the card on the box. So, we figured you would be okay with us checking who it was from rather than just opening the box. You know security protocols, Serg."

It was a gift from Paul Newman. Wow, the box contained a Grand Prix jacket and an Indy jersey signed by none other than Mr. Newman. His card said. "Thanks again big fella. My legs couldn't have done it without you. Stay healthy and keep the Mayor safe Rod Grimes."

Chapter 40
Run With The Vice President

The G-7 summit was in town, another big win for the city of Detroit. This a four-day meeting of the leaders from the seven advanced nations. Both the President and the Vice President were here in town and the city was in the international spotlight. Secret Service had this town on knockdown. The Mayor only delivered welcoming remarks on day one and his role was over.

On day three, the Vice President accepted an invitation to go for a morning run with the Mayor. Along with our Commanding Officer I met with the Secret Service advance team to go over the route for the run. It was decided we would use Belle Isle, which happened to be one of our regular running areas. The agents had some concerns about the number of citizens that visit the Isle daily, so a decision was made to close the Isle the night before their early morning run.

5:45 am, we arrived at the designated starting point on the six and half mile island. 6:00 am on the nose, three black Ford Crown Vic's pulled up. I was thinking that this must be the full advance team arriving before the Vice President. The doors opened and to my surprise, one of the people was the Vice President. The Mayor walked over to greet him and engaged in small talk while stretching.

The Vice President turned and asked, “So, who will be setting the pace this morning?” I raised my hand proudly and said, “It will be me sir.” He walked over to me and put his arm around my shoulder and casually led me away from the group. “What is your name?" he asked. "Sergeant Grimes, Sir," was my reply. "No, no, what is your name?" he asked again. This time I responded, "Rod sir." "Rod, I know your Mayor is a much faster runner than I am. I know he runs seven-minute miles. Even though I run the same distance as the Mayor, I can't run the three miles at his speed." "I understand sir. What kind of pace would you like?" "Rod," he said, "I am more like a nine minute per mile guy. There's no way I can hang with the Mayor's pace." "Not to worry sir. I will take care of you." "Great Rod. I was hoping I could count on you. The last thing I need is to run out of gas half way through the run. Then I would have to listen to your boss every time I see him. He will be talking trash to me about how he ran me into the ground." "No sir, he is my boss but we can't have that. You are the Vice President." We both smiled and walked back to rejoin the others.

The run went off without a hitch. We completed the three miles and afterwards the Vice President came over to me, shook my hand and said, "Thanks Rod, for taking care of me." We all got back into our cars and drove off.

Little did I know how much that meant to him; however, I would learn how special my little adjustment on pace would mean to the Vice President and how he would show his gratitude.

I remember being in Washington D.C. with the Mayor for a conference of Mayors and the Vice President made an appearance. I was positioned on a wall near where the Mayor was seated when the Vice President walked into the banquet room. He was shaking hands as the different Mayors wanted to get their face time with him. He looked over, saw me standing there, and headed straight towards me. "Rod, or should I be official and say Sergeant Grimes?" joking. "How are you?" he asked. Really, is this really happening? The Vice President of the United States just came over and spoke to me by my first name. No one is going to believe this. Wow! "Is there anything you need?" he continued. "Are they taking care of you?" "Yes sir, all is well on my end. Thank you for asking sir." As he turned to walk away, "Of course, you are my guy," giving me a head nod and an eye wink. The Vice President would demonstrate his kindness every time we crossed paths. He would make it a point to come over and speak and make sure I was well taken care of. That's something I will tell my grand kids about.

Chapter 41
Auto Show With A Foot Of Snow

Winter had set in again in the motor city. The holidays had just passed, and now just a few more months to spring. Before we got there, the cold fury of January and February awaited us.

The best thing about January in Detroit is the North America International Auto Show. The ten day show of all the new model cars and even the concept cars will be on display. If they build it anywhere in the world, we get to see it here at this massive show.

The show opens every year with a charity review. It's a black-tie event so the political and filthy rich can come together and mingle. I suspect, but can't prove anything, it is where some questionable deals are made. Maybe this is why the weather is always terrible.

That year was no exception. Fourteen inches of snow had fallen in the last two days and today, going into the night, we were expecting another five inches. The traffic was going to be a nightmare.

4:00 pm and the Mayor was ready to go home to get ready for this evening's gala. The normal twelve-minute drive from the office to his residence took 55 minutes, and the roads were only getting worse. 5:45 pm, and we were headed back downtown with the Mayor and the Mrs. What a terrible weather day for the black-tie event for the auto show.

The mayor handled his duties while spending a few hours previewing many of the new cars and concept vehicles. He looked my way and gave the nod that he had had enough and was ready to get out of here. Our departure took about thirty more minutes as people wanted to get their goodbyes in with the Mayor. We finally made it to the vehicle at 9:50 pm, and I knew the less than 10-mile drive would take more than an hour.

The snow had not let up and the plows just couldn't keep up. Several cars had been abandoned along our route, causing us to make adjustments to our route. Twice, I had to get out and push to get us unstuck. Ten minutes to midnight and we finally made it to our turn leading to the mansion. There was no way we could get the car down this street. The Mayor got out with me this time as I attempted to get us unstuck again, this time to no avail. After a couple of attempts, the Mayor said, "Let's walk the rest of the way." The Mrs. couldn't help but laugh, "There's no way I can walk in these heels." "Okay honey, you wait here with Officer Thompson. Rod and I will walk down to the house and get your snow boots."

It was a good thing the street is primarily used for the residents to get onto Jefferson and it was late. The last thing I wanted was for someone, even his neighbors, to see the predicament we were in and more so, the first lady having to walk home. We did what we had to do and all worked out fine. As time passed, the Mayor would jokingly bring up the time the first lady wore a formal dress and winter snow boots. Not to be outdone, she would fire back at him, "Yes, it was because you couldn't get the streets cleared Mr. Mayor."

Chapter 42

London, England And A Visit With The Queen

The year was 1999, and the Mayor was headed to London, England, for the American Bar Association Annual Convention. This would turn out to be the last time I would travel with the Mayor.

"Grimes," the Commanding Officer called out to me as I was walking back into the lobby. "I need to see you in my office." As we walked towards his office he said, "The boss really likes having you with him when he travels." We made it to his office and closed the door. He rubbed his hands together as he sat down behind his desk.

"The Mayor and first lady will be traveling to London; England and he requested you for the security detail." A huge smile came across my face in my mind. I forced myself not to outwardly show any emotions. "This will be an eight-day trip. The American Conference of Mayors have chosen to meet there. You know the drill; you will not be carrying a firearm so make sure you brush up on your non-weapon skills." That brought a laugh from both of us. We practiced that stuff every week. "You will leave in two weeks. Now I have to go and tell the other sergeants they were skipped over for this assignment. You really know how to make my job hard," as he stood up smiling before busting out in a loud laugh.

I arrived at the airport with two pieces of luggage feeling like I had over packed. I got checked in and waited for the arrival of the

Mayor and first lady. The car pulled up to the curb for international departures. I had notified the airport police of his traveling. Two uniformed officers stood by as we unloaded the luggage from the trunk. I was much relieved when Mrs. had four bags and the Mayor had three.

The Mayor greeted me as he did most of the time, "Sir Roderick, how are you doing on this fabulous morning?" I replied, "I am well sir. What a great day to fly." That was a code we used to let him know everything was all set inside and he could go straight through to our departing gate or to the VIP lounge. We had a little more than an hour before boarding, so he chose the latter.

Once we boarded the plane, they went to their seat in first class. I was heading to business class when one of the flight attendants waved for me to come over to where she was standing. "Are you traveling with the Mayor?" she asked. I hesitated to respond. "I know, I know you are not supposed to reveal that information. Now you may have to kill me." We both smiled and laughed at her humor. "Yes, yes, I am escorting him." "Well, I can't have you in another part of the plane. You need to be up here in first class so you can keep an eye on him, but more importantly, I can keep an eye on you." She identified an unassigned seat and redirected me with a smile. Wow, that was a clear signal that she was flirting and it made me blush a little. "Well, thank you for ensuring that the Mayor will be protected throughout this flight." The flight was more than seven hours and my new friend made sure I was comfortable throughout the trip. She was even interested in meeting for drinks later that evening. As much as I would have liked to carry on as if this was a pleasure trip, I remained professional and advised her that although the invitation was tempting, I had to decline. I was on duty for the entire trip. She understood and asked for my phone. I put my cell phone in her hand and she typed in all of her contact information, saying, "When you are back home and not on duty, please call and let's talk about that drink."

We landed in London, gathered our nine pieces of luggage, flagged a taxi, loaded up and headed to the hotel. I was expecting to hear a wise crack from the Mayor, but it came from the first lady. "Why Roderick, I think that flight attendant wanted to get familiar with you on a very personal level." Now, I was really blushing to hear this coming from the first lady. "Yes madam, she was not being shy at all," was the only reply I could come up with. The Mayor kept his face buried in the newspaper he had purchased on our way to the taxi stand, but his slight giggle let me know that he found the whole thing funny. I was sure he would get his digs in when his wife was not around.

London is a busy city, similar to New York. The 10-mile drive to the hotel took almost an hour. We got settled in, then met in the lobby and walked a few blocks over to a restaurant for dinner. Fish and chips were ordered around the table. They enjoyed a bottle of wine and I enjoyed iced tea that I couldn't get sweet enough.

At 5:45 am, the Mayor and I were up and headed out the door for his three-mile run. Damn! This was the worst part of my day. Twenty-five minutes later, we were walking back inside the hotel lobby. "Good run," he said with a silly grin on his face. "I will see you back here in the lobby in an hour."

The itinerary for the first full day was filled with short meetings and greet sessions at the hotel. He was done by 3:00 pm. He and the first lady filled the afternoon and evening in the shopping district near the hotel.

The next morning, we did our run, returned to the hotel and had breakfast before the shuttle bus arrived to take us to an event with the Prime Minister. Wow! I was going to meet Tony Blair, the Prime Minister. As soon as we stepped off our bus, the Secretary of State, Madeline Albright, was coming off her bus. The Mayor walked right over and greeted her but not without introducing me. The four of us posed for a picture. As the day went on, I met more city Mayors than I could remember. There were Congressmen and other high-profile dignitaries everywhere we went. Finally, we arrived back at our hotel shortly after 8:00 pm. There was a reception in the ballroom just off the lobby. Damn, we were not done yet. The first lady kept moving towards the elevator known as the lift in England. As she and the Mayor separated, she jokingly said, "I will see you in a few hours." I was praying that it was only a few minutes. Luck was with me. He made a quick walk through the room and upstairs we headed.

The alarm clock was ringing seemingly just minutes after my eyes closed. It was time to dress and head out for the worst thirty minutes of my day, our three-mile run. Like clockwork, the Mayor's door opened and I was standing there trying to act as if I was excited to be headed out to run three miles.

Day two took us to St. Paul's Cathedral. Wow! The architectural design is breathtaking. I am not usually moved by the design of buildings but this church was so amazing it was hard for me to not act like a total tourist.

Days three and four were for the delegation to do their own thing; heck, on day three, we didn't even run. It was nice that I got to sleep in until eight thirty am, which was good because my body was struggling to adjust to the time change.

After a late breakfast, we took to the streets of London for shopping. After the fourth store, the Mrs. said, "Rod, now you know why I brought an extra piece of luggage." "Yes ma'am, I see," I replied with a laugh. We returned to the hotel, dropped the bags and went right back out. The Mayor wanted to go to the world-famous Grosvenor Casino in Russell Square.

The walk was only ten minutes from our hotel. We walked inside and were greeted by the Maître d. "Membership card," he requested. The Mayor explained that we were visiting and were not members. "Sorry sir, if you are not a member you can't enter. This is a member only casino."

Not to be denied, the Mayor asked, "How does one become a member? "It is simple sir," the Maître d replied with his strong British accent. "I will need your ID." The Mayor proudly pulled his wallet from his back pocket and produced his driver's license. The Maître d began to enter the information into their system. Suddenly, he stopped and gave the Mayor his driver's license back. "I cannot provide you with a membership sir. You do not qualify. "Really?" said the Mayor with a tone of disbelief. I was thinking that this man had huge clout in America, but he didn't meet the criteria to be a member of this casino. With a visible smirk on his face, "Your driver's license has expired. Do you have your passport?" he asked. "No, no. I don't walk around with my passport when I travel abroad." The Mayor turned to his wife and asked if she had her driver's license only to be told no.

The Mayor turned to walk away. "Just a moment sir," I said. I turned to the Maître d and presented my driver's license. He entered my information and a few moments later the printer spit out a gold card, my membership to the famous casino. I turned back to the Mayor and the Mrs., and taking full advantage of the moment I said, "Sir, would you and the first lady care to join me as guest of my exclusive club?" extending my arm so they could enter in front of me. Once inside, out of the ear sound of the Maître d, I said, "Mr. Mayor, you know I am not going to let you live this down. Number one, you have been walking around with an expired driver's license in your wallet for nine months. I get that oversight because you are driven everywhere you go, but secondly, I have a membership at a club you couldn't qualify for." He wanted to laugh but refused, so I laughed enough for the both of us.

Day five, this was the day we were going to Buckingham Palace, I couldn't believe I was about to be in the presence of the Queen of England. I have met three United States Presidents, but meeting the Queen, I placed right there with meeting Nelson Mandela and the Pope.

We waited nearly ninety minutes, and then that special moment came. The Queen graced us with her presence. We were given instructions on what to do and when to do it, and by no means should we offer our hand for her to shake.

As the Queen moved past our place in the procession, I offered up a short bow of the head from the neck. She moved past with a faint but pleasant smile for me. I could leave London and head back to the States, this had to be the highlight of this trip, so I thought.

Out in front of the palace, crowds gathered to watch the changing of the guard. We decided to stay and watch this spectacle. We stood patiently with thousands of bystanders, watching as the guards stood almost lifeless, like mannequins. Suddenly, there was the sound of trumpets; then several more guards came marching out through the large gates in front of the palace. One by one, they took their place next to the guard already posted. Once all of the relief guards were in place, the old guards formed two columns and marched inside the gates. Once they were inside, the gates closed. It was worth the wait to see the precision of their movements. Once things settled down, I went over and asked if I could take a picture with two of them and my request was granted. How cool is that, a picture with the palace guards.

Day six, we took our normal early morning run, the thirty minutes from hell as I refer to it. Seven twenty-five am, we were back at the hotel. "Sir Roderick, we will meet back here in about twenty minutes to have breakfast." "Okay Mr. Mayor, I will see you then."

After breakfast, the buses were waiting for the next stop, the Palace of Westminster. This is equivalent to our House of Congress. We spent the entire afternoon there, listening to their lawmakers discuss various issues.

Day Seven started just as most, our run, then breakfast. Today's event was quite relaxing for the delegation. We spent most of the morning and afternoon at Hyde Park, the same park we do our three-mile run. At some point, the Mayor managed to get himself invited to the Prime Minister's residence for dinner.

At 6:00 pm sharp, a limo arrived at our hotel. The Mayor, first lady and I climbed in and off to 10 Downing Street we went. Unbelievable, I was about to have dinner at the Prime Minister of England's residence. This is equivalent to the White House in America. During the ride over, the Mayor shared with me that this is definitely one event I would want to lock in my memory. "You are about to have dinner in a historic dining room where less than 50 black men have ever dined." Given that insight, I locked that evening deep into my many special memories of this trip, and life memories for that matter. What an amazing way to end our visit overseas.

Day eight was all about getting paced and prepared to depart and come home. The buses arrived at the hotel shortly after 1:00 pm and I made sure all of the luggage was accounted for and loaded. As we boarded the plane, I thought to myself, "You have to have one of the best jobs ever."

Chapter 43

The Mayor Makes His Decision Not to Run for Reelection

The Mayor had planned his vacation, and there was something different about this one. Both of his adult sons were traveling with him and the first lady. Additionally, he was not taking any of the details with him, which told me there was going to be some serious family business discussed. I was guessing the subject of whether or not he would seek a third term in office would dominate this trip.

All potential candidates must make their intentions known by the end of the second week in July. The 10-day vacation went by in a flash. The detail took advantage of the downtime and caught up on some training.

My crew was on duty the second day the family arrived back home. I was on the main floor checking in with the maintenance man when the first lady walked into the kitchen. "Good morning," she spoke with a tone of joy in her voice and a glow on her face. I finished up with my business and retreated back downstairs to our security command office. My crew was getting prepared for our tour of duty. I told them to take a seat; I needed to tell them something. I started by saying, "We are a great team. We must continue to stay sharp and never let our guards down, no matter what." My officers could tell that this was not going to be a normal briefing. "What's up Sgt.?" one of them asked. "I don't have this as official information, but I can tell you that the Mayor will not be running for re-election." The room was silent for a few moments. "What! Why are you saying that? Did he tell you that?" "No, the

Mayor did not tell me anything, but the first lady told me. Now before you start spreading this around let me be clear about something."

"I have been with this family for about 10 years now. I know them very well, their behavior, facial expressions, tone of voice and other behaviors. I just saw the Mrs. upstairs in the kitchen. Although she didn't say the words and nor was there even a conversation about it, her presence said everything. The tone in her voice and the glow on her face said it all. See, I knew the reason no security went on their vacation, which has never happened before. The fact that both adult sons went with them told me that the family was going to make a decision about the future, and she clearly expressed what that decision was by her glow. No more dealing with the lies about her husband, no more sitting quietly by while citizens show little to no respect for what he is trying to do to bring this city back. Yes, she told me without saying a word about it."

"Let's continue to do our job to the best of our ability, and start thinking about the next assignment you may be interested in working on. The new Mayor will bring his own team in but will keep a few of us around to help with the transition. That time may be short lived so be prepared. If I am wrong that would be great, but I don't think I am."

Nearly three months had passed, and one day was the day the Mayor must make his intentions known. He had a press conference scheduled for twelve noon at one of the housing project complexes located on the east side. That day, I decided to be the jump man in the car with the Mayor. I was hip pocket, and if anything was going to go down, I wanted to be the person handling him.

We arrived on site at 11:15 am with the first lady at his side. His two sons and their spouse and girl arrived a few minutes later. By 11:30 am, all of his family was there in the hold room with us. The crowd was growing with both, those that wanted him to run and some that didn't. All of the news outlets were setting up television, radio and print. This announcement was going to be the biggest story of the day no matter which way he went.

It was time for the family to take their place in the audience. The room cleared and now it was just the Mayor and me in the room. He had about ten minutes to gather his thoughts. I stood quietly by the door as he paced back and forth. I knew he was struggling with something.

"Mr. Mayor, are you okay?" I asked. "Sir Roderick," he said with a quiet voice. "I have a written statement in each of my breast pockets. One says I am running, and the other says I am not, I am torn." "There is a part of me that knows I have more to do and I have the energy to take on the challenges. There is a part of me that is saying it is time to step down and relieve my family from all of the madness of being Mayor."

"Sir, if I may, can I speak freely?" "Of course Rod, please do. You have been with me from the very beginning and I would like to hear your thoughts." "Sir, I have watched you pour your heart and soul into this city. I have watched you take insults and unnecessary abuse from many, including several members of City Council. I have been with you 10 years, many of those days were twenty-hour days. I got to go home and recover, but you had to get up and do it all over in a few short hours. For personal reasons, I would jump for joy if your decision is to run again. I know the city would be better off having you continue at the helm. I could continue to serve in my capacity, which has been amazing, that part is my own selfish reason. If you choose to not run again, I totally understand and will be right here with you to the very end. Your family has endured so much unnecessary abuse and hate, so if you want to take that pain away from them, I support you with that decision as well. Whatever you decide when you walk out there, I want you to know it has been an honor and a privilege to serve on your protection detail. Every day I was on duty I was prepared to lay my life on the line to ensure that you made it home to the first lady. So when you walk out there and tell the world your intentions, just know that I am proud of you."

We were interrupted by a soft knock on the door. I opened the door and his press person stepped inside. "It's time sir."

The Mayor walked out to the podium where several mic phones are positioned and delivered a very heartfelt statement and shared with the world that he would not seek a third term.

Chapter 44
The Interview

The months were counting down and this assignment was coming to an end. In less than two months, the new Mayor would take office and he would bring his security team with him. I was home relaxing on my day off when the phone rang. To my surprise, it was the Sergeant that was running the Mayor Elect security team. "Hey Rod. How's it going?" he asked. "I wanted to give you a call to see if you would be interested in coming in for an interview to work on the Mayor Elect's security team." Having firsthand knowledge of Mayor Elect's personality, deep down inside, I didn't have a good feeling about it, but I accepted the offer to interview. After all, I only had 14 months to go before I could retire, and being in this role for over 10 years, I admit that I was very comfortable with this assignment. Even though I knew my professionalism would be challenged every day I worked for the new guy, I could handle it as opposed to taking on a new assignment with new duties and responsibilities. That ideology was pretty selfish, so I agreed to come in for the interview.

A few days later, I was walking into the interview room. The Sergeant who called me and two other gentlemen I didn't know were sitting there. The Sergeant stood up and shook my hand as he greeted me. The other two kept their seats as I was introduced to them. "This is Officer Mason, and Officer Jones." "Officers," I thought, "why am I, a Sergeant, being interviewed by police officers that I outrank, and secondly, the nerve of them to not even stand up and greet me. After all, I am their superior officer." I was not feeling good already, but I would listen to what they had to say.

Sergeant Wilson started by thanking me for coming in and praising me for my professional service to the outgoing Mayor. "Rod. Let's be clear here. There is nothing we can teach you about this assignment, or tell you. You have been in this role for two terms. Quite frankly, we are asking you to come aboard to teach us how to be an effective operation." "Okay," I was thinking, "they do respect my experience and knowledge of this assignment." I was not prepared for what he said next. "Officer Mason will be named the Commanding Officer and Officer Jones will be second in command." I sat there almost in shock. "Are you saying you will have police officers in charge of this detail and Sergeants will be reporting to them?" "Yes Rod. That is the direction the Mayor Elect is going." "Does the Mayor Elect plan on promoting them to the rank of Sergeant once he takes office?" was my first question. "No, they will remain in the rank of Police Officers."

Now I was confused as to how in the hell this was going to work, so I asked, "Are you telling me that the Mayor Elect plans on having Sergeants' report to Police Officers? This department has rank structure for a reason. What happens if there is a need for disciplinary action? How does a police officer discipline a person of a higher rank? The unions will have a field day with this. With no disrespect to you Mason and Jones, there is no way in hell I am going to let a police officer tell me what to do. I have earned these stripes and the responsibilities that come with them." "Rod, don't get so excited. They will follow your lead. We need you here to help shape the new team." "Well, why am I not being interviewed by someone of a higher rank for the position of Commanding Officer over the detail? Never mind, there is no need to answer that question. This operation is all about friends and family hookups and I am not interested in being a part of this foolishness. Thank you for the invite, but no thank you." I stood up and, shook Sergeant Wilson's hand and walked out of the room without acknowledging the other two. As it turned out, Officers Mason and Jones were close friends with the Mayor Elect and the future Mayor wanted his boys close to him. It wasn't long after that information surfaced about Officer Mason's discipline troubles. He was about to be fired for having a number of discipline issues in his short four-year career.

Chapter 45
The Final Days on the Detail

It was December; we were down to the wire; the Mayor only had a few weeks left to serve his term. The holiday events didn't have the same feel to them. Staff members knew they would have to look for new jobs within the city's management structure. Some would find themselves out of a job altogether. The security detail doesn't have that to worry about. We were members of the police department so we would just be assigned to another unit within the department.

No one was in a festive mood, not even the Mayor. Everyone was just trying to get these last two weeks over. Boxes and boxes of files and personal belongings were being hauled out every day. The Mayor had spent eight years in his role and had collected tons of memorabilia and other items that needed to be removed.

It was New Year's Eve, the last official day for the Mayor. In addition to getting the office cleaned out, the family also had to pack up items from the residence as it, too is property of the city and designated as the Mayor's residence. The keys to the office were turned over to the incoming detail yesterday. I had the pleasure of being on shift when the Mayor took office eight years ago, and it was my honor and privilege to be there on his last day.

The day was speeding by at warp speed. We made sure that the last boxes were collected by the movers at the Manoogian Mansion and taken to their new home. It was a little after 10:00 pm and the first family was preparing to go to midnight mass for the last time in their current official capacity.

While en route to the church, the Mayor advised me that there were still a few boxes in the mayor's office and he wanted to stop by and retrieve them after church service. The Mayor asked me to reach out to the new detail to see if someone could meet us there around 12:30 am so we could get the last of the boxes. I placed a call in to Sergeant Wilson and he returned it while services were still going on. I stepped out and took his call. I advised him that the outgoing Mayor still had a couple of boxes in the office and we would like someone to meet us there to let us in to get them. He said that shouldn't be a problem but let him check with the new Mayor. Sergeant Wilson called me back a few minutes later and shocked me with his answer that it would not be possible for us to come by tonight. "Really," I replied. "This will only take about two minutes. Can't you help me out on this?" Sergeant Wilson said, "Rod, you know if it was my call it would happen without a second thought, but when I told the Mayor Elect of your request he said no, and had a few unpleasant remarks to go with his answer. The only thing I can do, Rod, is put the boxes in the security office and hold them there until you or someone can pick them up once the Mayor's office reopens in the New Year."

Once church service was over, I advised the Mayor of the answer to his request. I told him that it was not going to happen tonight and we would have to wait until next week to pick the boxes up. The Mayor was somewhat shocked, then slightly irritated. "What reason was given that we can't stop by and get them tonight?" he asked. "Sir, please, just let me stop by and get them next week. My contact promised that he will secure them until then."

"Roderick, just tell me why we can't go tonight. What was his reason?" "I didn't want to tell you this sir, but a quote from the new Mayor." "tell that motherfucking former Mayor that we will be up in that bitch partying at 12:01 am, so no he can't come and get shit' was what I was told." The hurt on his face cut me like a knife, and there was nothing I could do about it. The ride home was in complete silence.

We arrived back at their new residence and I walked them inside. The former first lady thanked me for my service with tears in her eyes, gave me a hug and walked into another room. I turned to the Mayor, fighting back tears myself. I said, "Sir, it has been my honor to serve on your detail for all eight years. On behalf of the entire detail, we thank you for your service, dedication and leadership, making this city a better place for our citizens." I gave him a final salute. He also thanked me for my service in keeping him and his family safe for two terms. With that being said, I walked out the door and stood there until I heard the locks click on the door. The tears began to flow uncontrollably.

Chapter 46
Eastern Operations

Leading up to the end of my assignment in the mayor's office, I had secured a position working in one of the Deputy Chief's office. My new role was assisting the Deputy Chief responsible for running the Districts on the east side of the city, as well as three additional sections operating on the east side.

The Deputy Chief was my good friend who was the Sergeant that recommended me to volunteer on the campaign 10 years ago. It was an easy transition into the assignment as a result of our relationship.

My responsibilities were less stressful, but I did a lot of reading. I and another Sergeant split the precincts between us. Our job was to proofread every report that came into the Deputy Chief's office and make sure there were no errors in grammar. We also had to make sure that department policy and procedures were followed. After a few weeks I was a pro, but because of all of that reading, I now needed glasses.

Four months had passed, and things were going well. Then, the rug was pulled from under my feet. My Deputy Chief was reassigned to the Chief's office, but when asked if he could bring any of his staff with him, it was denied. The new Deputy Chief who replaced him brought his own staff with him, leaving me out in the cold.

More than two months passed and I still was not transferred to a new assignment. There was no place for me to sit, so I had to hang out in the break room. I was in total limbo. My old Deputy

Chief had nowhere for me to work, and the new Deputy Chief had nothing for me to do. I would show up each morning, go to the break room, read the paper, and watch Sports Center on the television until around 11:00 am. I would go take the Deputy Chief's car, get it washed and gassed up, then take about an hour for lunch. I would come back to the office and sit around until around 2:00 pm when the boss would stick his head in and tell me, "I will see you tomorrow."

This was easy money for me, but eventually, it became a bore and a total waste of personnel. What's even crazier, the Deputy Chief started asking me each day if I had heard anything about a new assignment. I was thinking, "Why are you asking me? You're the boss, make some calls and get me out of here."

Finally, I received a call from the Chief's office that I had been officially transferred to another assignment.

Chapter 47
Missing Reserves

Next stop in my career, I was assigned to second in command over the Reserve's Unit. My former Deputy Chief had restructured that unit and as luck would have it, the Lieutenant he put in charge was that little lady who looked like a school teacher from my academy class and the first partner I walked the beat with. Here we are reunited again. The Deputy Chief told me he had been working on making this happen for more than a month and having me in the role would allow him access to me as he needed me. I was cool with it; I just wish he had communicated what he was doing instead of leaving me hanging.

The Lieutenant had spent a number of years assigned to the medical section, which didn't give her much experience in managing a unit.

Our department had over five hundred people on the books serving as Police Reserves. The reality was there were only about fifty to sixty reservists doing volunteer work. Over the years, they just stopped coming and putting in the required twenty hours per month to keep their status.

We began to revamp the unit. We started by first tracking down all of the individuals with badges and guns but not providing any service to the city. I had a team of five police officers assigned to me. We spent the next four months locating inactive reserves and getting them re-engaged or collecting our equipment and taking them off the books. We restructured the unit with four hundred twenty-three reserves. Then, the department had personnel available for non-emergency details at our disposal.

Chapter 48
Community Unity

It wasn't long after we had the unit restructured that the Deputy Chief had me come down to his office. He had just been given a monumental task. The Chief had just saddled him with the task of providing a plan to keep the auto show safe. This event happened every year in January for nine days. The last eight days are open to the public. This also just happened to be a winter break for schools. There were a number of gangs across the city and with them not mixing and mingling in the schools for a week, they took advantage of the auto show as their gathering spot. Kids fighting inside the exhibit and throughout the downtown area was common practice. The Chief wanted to get a handle on things but couldn't afford to pay overtime to properly staff such a high manpower event.

The Deputy Chief and I talked about how the reserve unit could help support the regular officers assigned but even that was not enough. I mentioned that this was a regional event and patrons came from all across southeast Michigan and beyond to attend the show. Maybe we could get support from the neighboring police agencies to assist; after all, it was their citizens from their communities as well.

The Deputy Chief ran the idea by the Chief, who said the city law department would have to sign off on bringing other officers into our jurisdiction. The idea was quickly shot down because of the liability.

I did some research and discovered that more than thirty police agencies in surrounding cities have reserve units. I shared this information with the Deputy Chief as a possible source of manpower. The reserves are civilians volunteering to perform non-emergency duties; therefore, the liability is no different than that of a Detroit reserve. The Deputy Chief took this idea to the law department and they approved the concept.

I began contacting police departments within a twenty-five-mile radius that had a reserve unit within their department. I shared the idea and pitched it as a multi-department initiative and how their city residents would have a greater sense of safety if they saw uniforms from their city helping keep things safe.

The first year, I sent the request to 24 departments asking for their assistance and 14 sent personnel from their reserve units. I partnered one of the suburban departments with a Detroit reserve officer. Not only did this give us the necessary personnel to keep the event safe, but the visiting reservist had a blast being a part of a Detroit event. Their citizens were very excited to see the unity of law enforcement working together.

A few months later, the Detroit Red Wings won the Stanley Cup and the city gave them a parade. My call went out to 32 departments and 25 sent their reserve officers. The word had spread and more departments wanted to be seen as team players. I used this strategy for the next several regional events - the Thanksgiving Day Parade, Detroit Pistons NBA Champions Parade, and Detroit Fireworks celebration. All became a big hit with our regional partners.

Chapter 49
Calling it Quits

Where did the years go? It was May 2002 and I was celebrating my 24 years since graduating from the police academy; nine more months and I could call it quits if I choose. The new Chief came to town and was being very disrespectful to the members of this department. If there is one thing I know about being a strong leader, it is to treat your subordinates with respect. A manager has to know when to crack the whip and when to spread the honey. This Chief only believed in keeping his foot on his officers' neck.

Nepotism was running wild in the Mayor's office. It was rumored that our new Chief was a cousin of the new first lady, that would be fine if he was qualified for the position. Not only did he fail to gain the confidence of the men and women in the department, he wouldn't even get his certification in the state of Michigan. Although the state certification issued by the Michigan Law Enforcement Council is not required to hold the title of police chief, he had no desire to take that five-day course.

He spent much of his time learning the social circles of Detroit rather than addressing the criminal elements. It was loosely being said that the new Mayor had little respect for the police department and he even gave a shout out to a gang operating in the neighborhood he grew up in. This kind of behavior was making policing a real challenge for the patrol officers. The Chief was busy on talk radio shows saying things like, "I am sick of these officers walking around here like they are going to a club instead of going to work." He went as far as to say the male officers are walking around in Stacey Adam dress shoes while in uniform, and the female officers are wearing pump heels. How offensive! The men and women suit up every day to go out and make a difference utilizing the limited resources available to them.

The morale had hit an all-time low. The administration and the Chief had torn down many of the bridges built by the previous administration with the police unions. I have always believed in coming to work and doing the best job possible, as did most of our officers. The straw that broke the camel's back for me was when the Chief directed officers to wear a pin on our uniform that read, "DPD, minding my own business." During a visit to the City Council for budget review, the Council President asked the Chief about the pins, questioned the meaning and if the statement was proper English. The Chief's response was, "It doesn't matter. Most of my officers only have GEDs." The truth of the matter, DPD personnel was one of the most educated departments in the nation. I knew it was time for me to start looking for a new job. I never thought I would see the day that my own leadership would be so embarrassing that I would rather leave than be humiliated.

Over the summer months, I began playing golf with my former Commanding Officer in the Mayor's office. He had retired a few years ago and was now the Executive Lieutenant at the Detroit Public Schools Public Safety Department. Other guys in that group were the Chief of the department and one of the Sergeants, all of which I have known for years and played softball.

One day, while on the course, the Lieutenant mentioned to the Chief how instrumental I was in making the protection detail a success while he was in charge. The next week, when we were on the golf course, the Chief asked me if I was interested in coming aboard his department. He was looking for someone with strong leadership skills who could assist with training. “Charlie, I mean Chief. That is something I would definitely consider. I still have seven months before I am eligible to retire.”

As the days and weeks in the summer of 2002 passed, DPD leadership continued its assault on its members and my thick skin was wearing thin. Week after week, while on the golf course, the Chief and the Lieutenant took turns asking me about coming over to their department. By the time September had rolled around, I had had enough of the disrespect from the leaders at DPD. The Lieutenant and I were riding in the same golf cart today and I told him that I had enough, come February 2003, I would be ready to transition over. Charlie was thrilled to hear the news as we all walked onto the 18th green.

“When can you start “Q”?” my future boss asked with excitement in his voice. “Well Charlie, I better get used to calling you Chief. I can start in five months. I can retire on February 20th, 2003, and be available after that.” “Great! That will give us time to talk about how you can best fit within my department.”

I left the golf course both excited and heartbroken. Excited because there was another department that was excited to have me come aboard, and heartbroken because the department that I love had made it just about unbearable to show up and give my all. Twenty-five years and I only used three sick days. Clearly, I was dedicated.

This department taught me so many life skills and provided me the opportunity to financially support myself. The thought of leaving on these terms was sickening. Over the years, I always remembered what my parents taught me to always follow my dreams. They also instilled in me to always be my best, no matter what I chose to do in life, and if I found myself unable to do that, then I should strongly consider doing something else.

February 21, 2003, I retired from the Detroit Police Department.

Epilogue

A genuine commitment to community service is a true calling, twenty five years of service to the city I love was just that. I know I have so much more to offer, but unfortunately continuing to serve in the Detroit Police Department was no longer an option for me.

The end

Made in United States
Orlando, FL
08 February 2024

43442151R00117